MW00676504

WHAT TEENAGERS ARE SAYING ABOUT

DRUGS & ALCOHOL

Campus Life Books

Against All Odds
Alive
Alive II
The Campus Life Guide to Dating
The Campus Life Guide to Making and Keeping Friends
The Campus Life Guide to Surviving High School
The Life of the Party
The Lighter Side of Campus Life
A Love Story
Peer Pressure: Making It Work for You
What Teenagers Are Saying About Drugs and Alcohol
Worth the Wait
You Call This a Family?

What Teenagers Are Saying About

Drugs & Alcohol

CHRIS LUTES

A DIVISION OF CTI
CampusLife
BOOKS

Zondervan Publishing House
Grand Rapids, Michigan

What Teenagers Are Saying About Drugs and Alcohol
Copyright © 1987, 1990 by Campus Life Books, a division of CTi
All rights reserved

Published by Zondervan Publishing House
1415 Lake Drive, S.E., Grand Rapids, Michigan 49506

Library of Congress Cataloging-in-Publication Data

Lutes, Chris
    What teenagers are saying about drugs & alcohol / Chris Lutes.
        p. cm.
    Reprint. Originally published: Wheaton, Ill. : Tyndale House,
1988.
    Summary: Uses a Christian perspective to present the views of
American teenagers on drugs and alcohol.
    ISBN 0-310-71051-0
    1. Teenagers—United States—Drug use. 2. Teenagers—United
States—Alcohol use. 3. Teenagers—United States—Attitudes.
[1. Drug abuse. 2. Alcohol. 3. Alcoholism.] I. Title.
[HV5824.Y68L88   1990]
362.29'11'0835—dc20   90–34688
                                                            CIP
                                                            AC

All Scripture quotations, unless otherwise noted, are taken from the *Holy Bible: New International Version* (North American Edition). Copyright © 1973, 1978, 1984, by the International Bible Society. Used by permission of Zondervan Bible Publishers.

All rights reserved. No part of this publication may be reproduced, stored in a retrieval system, or transmitted in any form or by any means—electronic, mechanical, photocopy, recording, or any other—except for brief quotations in printed reviews, without the prior permission of the publisher.

Printed in the United States of America

90 91 92 93 94 / CH / 5 4 3 2 1

CONTENTS

Parent ■ Living with Addiction in the Family ■ Survival
Skills

PART THREE
THE SEARCH FOR ANSWERS THAT WORK

INTRODUCTION

Fundamentally, this book is by teenagers. I have tried to keep my own observations to the minimum and let young people speak for themselves, for it is only by understanding teenage perspectives that we can understand the real meaning of America's drug crisis.

I hope reading this book will help you understand how teenagers feel—both those who use drugs and those who don't. As you read you will grasp their ambivalence about alcohol, hear their cynicism about solutions, and gain a realistic sense of what the problem is and what can and must be done about it.

In the fall of 1986, I sent out five different surveys covering a wide variety of open-ended questions to hundreds of high schools across the country. Some of the survey questions were:

Is there such a thing as a responsible use of drugs? *Explain.*
Is there such a thing as a responsible use of alcohol? *Explain.*
Why do teenagers use drugs?
Why do teenagers drink alcohol?
What are the most popular types of drugs at your school?
What are the most popular alcoholic beverages at your school?
How would you define the "drug problem"? Give examples to support your answer.
How would you define the "alcohol problem"? Give examples to support your answer.
What do you think is good or weak about current educational efforts to stop drug use? *Explain your answer.*

What would be the best way for a drug and alcohol program to really help people?

The surveys also had personal questions about the students' own drug use and drinking habits. Through the surveys (and many personal interviews), I probed students' motivations and reasons for using drugs and alcohol. In addition, I tried to understand why students choose not to use drugs and drink alcohol. All in all, I wanted to get beyond the startling statistics of the six o'clock news to discover what teens really think.

Eventually, more than five thousand completed surveys (about one thousand of each survey sent out) came in from more than one hundred schools across the country. Researcher Virginia Vagt—to whom I owe many thanks—added her expertise in tabulating and analyzing the data from those surveys. A research staff then chose a total of two hundred responses from each of the five surveys (one hundred males and one hundred females) and tabulated the findings. *Campus Life* magazine also included a survey in its September 1986 issue. Statistics and stories generated from the magazine survey went into my research. So, as you read, you will find not only facts and figures, but hundreds of quotes taken directly from those five thousand surveys.

To supplement the surveys, I crisscrossed America to do over thirty personal interviews and several group interviews. All of this student-generated material appears as short quotes and longer profiles, and is both reinforced and at times challenged by input from Gallup polls and other research.

To better understand the meaning behind what was written in the surveys and letters and what was said in the interviews, I have read various studies, books, and research data on teenage drug and alcohol use. All of this has gone into the analysis and interpretation in this book. I hope you will find such commentary helpful in understanding the drug and alcohol issues facing today's teenagers.

One other note: Because I wanted this book to be more than a "nice bit of research," it includes values and ethical perspectives. I do not apologize for any references to religion and the Christian faith. As a Christian, my faith plays an integral part in the way I look at life and in the way I understand the world around me. Interestingly enough, I have found that religion plays the same role in the perspectives expressed by many high school students. It would be irresponsible not to include those perspectives, particularly since much of the student input on religious viewpoints came to me from letters sent to *Campus Life* magazine.

I wish to thank all of the students who through interviews, letters, and surveys took part in the creation of *What Teenagers Are Saying about Drugs and Alcohol*. This book is as much theirs as mine.

Chris Lutes, August 1987

PART ONE

LOOKING BENEATH THE SURFACE

O N E

TEENAGERS AND DRUGS

WHO IS USING?

Massachusetts Governor Michael Dukakis surveyed 5,000 of his state's high school students in 1984 and found that 60 percent admitted having used illegal drugs. (Newsweek, *August 11, 1986*)

In the largest drug-use survey ever undertaken, over 200,000 sixth-through twelfth-grade children admitted to behavior that would horrify their parents—if they knew. Our children are using drugs in ever-increasing numbers and at younger and younger ages. They're popping pills and smoking pot on the school bus, getting drunk in their cars and at friends' houses, and even snorting cocaine in their own homes. (Family Circle, *September 24, 1985*)

Drug education gets an F. (Story headline, U.S. News & World Report, *October 13, 1986)*

Like most Americans, I read the newspapers and watch the evening news. In the past few years, I have seen drug abuse take its moment in the spotlight. And quite a moment it has been. Heavy black headlines and TV commentators' dramatic voices addressed such unsettling and sensational topics as: "Drugs: The Enemy Within," "America on Drugs," and "The Drug Crisis." Through all the media hoopla, peer pressure became trumpeted as a major cause of drug use, parents' use of drugs and alcohol became a major concern, failed educational programs received their share of condemnation, and athletes became fallen—and sometimes dead—role models.

The Reagan administration joined in the battle against drug abuse, with Nancy Reagan championing her "Just Say No" campaigns. Movie stars came along and tried to use their own types of anti-drug persuasion to sway the nation's young. Almost ironically, news coverage became upbeat, with a few "news behind the news" stories about teenagers who vocally proclaimed their aversion to drug use.

Amid it all there have been occasional (albeit short and guarded) stories offering perspective and hope. In its September 15, 1986, cover story, *Time* stated: "In 1978, according to government surveys, a staggering 10 percent of all high school seniors smoked marijuana every day. Today the percentage has dropped by half. That is still way too high, but attitudes have changed markedly. [In 1978] only one-quarter of high school seniors reported that marijuana was a dangerous drug . . . but now fully 75 percent do." Then in its March 9, 1987, issue, *Time* again offered cautiously optimistic words: "The statistics are nothing to celebrate: 58 percent of high school seniors admit to having tried illegal drugs at least once. But the percentages of students experimenting with drugs actually dropped last year, as it has every year but one since 1978."

Pollster George Gallup also offered reasons for optimism when a 1987 Gallup youth survey stated that "only 1 percent of U.S. teens have tried crack." And Gallup's 1986 research showed a decline in marijuana use from year to year (with the exception of 1983).

CHART 1 **TRENDS IN ACCEPTANCE AND USE OF MARIJUANA**

	1986	1985	1983	1981	1979
Ever Used Marijuana	24%	23%	19%	37%	41%
Used in Past Month	6%	8%	8%	13%	27%

Source: *THE GALLUP YOUTH SURVEY* (1986). Used by permission from the Associated Press.

Throughout all the media coverage, I have been well aware of the bad image given to the nation's youth. I have also noticed a couple of important deletions:

1. *Teenagers are talked about but rarely talked to.* A noteworthy exception to this concern is the work by adviser Howard Spanogle and his journalism students from Glenbard East High School in Lombard, Illi-

nois. Spanogle and his teenage staff produced a book appropriately called *Teenagers Themselves* (New York: Adama Books, 1984) in which students voice their views and opinions on a variety of topics, including drug abuse. Still, for the most part, teenagers as sources and resources are left out except to use them for "cold, formal research," which many resent. Said one skeptical student who filled out a *Campus Life* survey, "If this is to collect a lot of stats to scare people, it probably won't do any good."

2. *Alcohol use is largely overlooked.* For the most part, the current "Just Say No" campaigns ignore alcohol. The otherwise fine handbook from the U.S. Department of Education *What Works: Schools without Drugs* ignores alcohol abuse. The media largely overlook the use of alcohol, while focusing on "street drugs." Although many experts do not see alcohol as a traditional drug, none of them disputes its potentially dangerous effects and drug-like qualities. One *Chicago Tribune* article (another notable exception) labeled alcohol and cigarettes as "gateway drugs that lead to illicit drug use for many adolescents."

My initial concern in writing *What Teenagers Are Saying about Drugs and Alcohol* came out of the enormous void and *avoidance* of the perspective and viewpoint of young people. As an editor for *Campus Life*, a youth magazine, I am always concerned that young people be given the opportunity to speak for themselves. I do not believe we can possibly begin to know what is happening out there unless we get with the insiders. The ways we can gain insight into teenage drug and alcohol use and abuse are through allowing teenagers to talk, profiling many individual concerns, and avoiding the shortcomings of creating a composite picture of the "typical teenager."

It's too easy to group those with drug problems as "druggies," "stoners," and "dopers," but such labels keep us from getting close enough to see their pain, potential, and value as human beings. It also, as the media have so deftly demonstrated, fosters negative attitudes and stereotypes.

IS EVERYBODY GETTING BUZZED?

As I began my research, I wanted to find out how students felt about the drug and alcohol issue in their own schools and communities. Did they see these as problems? Or did they think the media had blown the issue totally out of proportion? The varied answers I received were from the students' own experiences and perceptions, based on personal or *subjective* observations rather than on *objective* facts. For instance, one young girl wrote, "I can almost bet that 95 percent of our school has tried some sort of illegal drug. I think that's irresponsible and completely stupid." Chances are, judging by national statistics, her estimate is excessive. Yet, her *feelings* about the problem at her school are very important. Most likely her own experience tells her that usage is much higher than it should be.

Gallup surveys offer some interesting insight into the difference between perception and fact. As quoted in the beginning of this chapter, a 1987 Gallup survey indicated that "only 1 percent of U.S. teens say they have tried crack (a smokable form of cocaine)." However, the same survey also stated that "three teens in four say they believe there are at least some students at their school who have tried crack. This includes 5 percent who estimated that a 'very large number' have used it, and 55 percent who think only a few students have tried it. One teen in five (21 percent) believes there are no students at his school who have tried crack, while 5 percent say they don't know if any have used the substance." It should also be pointed out that more girls (18 percent) than guys (9 percent) think a "fairly large number" have tried crack. Girls perceive cocaine usage to be more widely spread than guys do.

These are measurements of perception. More on the factual level (assuming that the students are being honest about their own use) are the responses to the *Campus Life* survey questions, "Have you ever used drugs?" and "Are you currently using drugs?" One out of every four (27 percent) teens who responded said they have at one time or another used drugs. One out of ten said they currently use some kind of illegal drug. While that may not seem like a large number who are currently using, let's bring it down to a practical level. In a classroom of thirty, three students could be using some kind of illegal substance. Three possibly disruptive students—or even one—can make it seem as though "95 percent of our school has tried some sort of illegal drug."

What Students Say Is Happening on Campus

Here are some of the ways students perceive the drug and alcohol problem in their own schools and communities. I have included a large number of quotes to give you a feel for the varying voices of teenagers, almost as though you were listening in on a high school discussion.

"People think you're weird if you don't do drugs" (Female, 19, Colorado).

"The alcohol problem is even worse than the drug problem because students believe it is less serious" (Male, 14, Missouri).

GRAPH 1

Have you ever used drugs?

YES	50%	100%

■■■■■ **27%**

NO

■■■■■■■■■■■■ **73%**

Are you currently using drugs?

YES

■■■ **10%**

NO

■■■■■■■■■■■■■ **90%**

The 1986 *CAMPUS LIFE* survey of high school students.

"In my three long years at [name of school] I have seen a major decline in drug abuse, but an increase in alcohol. I think this is a positive thing" (Male, 16, Virginia).

"I don't like it when parents think that all kids are hooked on drugs. A lot of kids are not. I do not want people looking down at me because some kids are bad" (Male, 15, California).

"I believe alcohol and drugs are a major problem in our school system today. I think something ought to be done about it. Soon! Before more lives are taken" (Female, 16, Virginia).

"I know of two people who deal drugs here, and I am sure there are dozens more" (Female, 17, Ohio).

"Alcohol and drugs are both pretty popular at my school. About 99 percent have at least tried one or the other (my guess), about 75 percent (also my guess) drink or take drugs regularly (at least once a week). Many people from my school have been to drug rehab centers for a few weeks" (Female, 16, Iowa).

"I go to a private Catholic school, but things aren't much different here than in other schools. Our school was recently surveyed on the drug and alcohol problem, and we fit the national statistics. Our problem is the same as anybody else's" (Female, 18, Chicago).

"Students today seem to be labeled. Not everyone uses drugs and not everyone drinks. I think this needs to be pointed out. We are not all bad. Somebody needs to take a look around" (Female, 16, Texas).

"I really don't think teenagers realize how serious the alcohol and drug problem is" (Female, 16, Washington).

"I know that everybody here is smoking pot and getting drunk. I was kind of surprised because down in California, where I used to live, it's really different. Most everybody down there just smokes cigarettes. Down there alcohol and drugs weren't a very big factor. It was for some people, but not very often. Then I came up here and it's been really weird. Kind of a big change" (Male, 17, Washington).

"I know there are a lot of problems with drugs here, but there is also help through groups like SADD" (Female, 15, Illinois).

"I'd say 98 percent of the kids at this school have tried marijuana, 20 to 30 percent are daily users, and about 60 to 75 percent use it on the weekends. In terms of growing popularity, however, it's not as much pot anymore. People are doing more cocaine, more acid now. I was talking to a friend of mine who deals with a guy who brings it into the country. He deals straight with this dealer at the airport, and he said that the same people who were selling pot before are selling cocaine now" (Male, 17, Illinois).

"Drinking and drugs aren't very in at this school" (Female, 16, California).

"The first day I was at this school I was approached twice by people [who wanted me] to buy drugs" (Male, 18, Ohio).

"Throughout high school I have been around [kids who] drink. The majority of the school drinks on weekends. Now I find that drinking has begun in the middle school. Drinking is a serious risk, and something should be done to shock young people into realizing what they are getting into" (Female, 17, South Carolina).

"In my school I know a lot of people who do pot. I know there are some doing cocaine, but I don't know how many. In this area there aren't many hard users that I know of. But since I'm not a user or anything, I don't come in contact with these people too often, but I am friends with them. I go to parties and people are smoking joints all over the place" (Female, 16, Missouri).

"Alcohol is a huge problem, bigger than any adult knows or understands. It's pretty bad when 95 percent of my class's student council and 95 percent of all athletes at my school drink" (Female, 16, Ohio).

"All the surveys that have been given in high schools should not be taken seriously as they have been. If an adult really thinks that 75 percent of a school takes drugs on a regular basis, they are really close-minded, because that is not possible. School officials need to look at the school and students individually, not at what they write on an absurd survey. I can assure any adult that asks me that I don't believe America's teenagers are as hooked on drugs and on alcohol as they think" (Female, 15, Texas).

"Most people get the impression that only scum smoke pot or do drugs. It's not true. People who are considered normal are on drugs, but they can hide it better" (Female, 16, Wisconsin).

"The drug problem is bad, but I do not believe the majority of teens fall into this category. The bad get the spotlight instead of the good. I also feel that alcohol is a worse problem than drugs because it is publicized as socially acceptable: 'Turn it loose tonight—Coors Light,' 'Head for the mountains—head for Busch Beer,' 'Bring out your best—Budweiser Light.' And watch all these ads—what do you see? The prettiest girls, the best-looking guys, and they seem to be having the time of their lives. To many teens who are already confused, this seems to be a way out—the way to have fun.

"Even so, I can't name that many people who drink or use drugs. Looking at the ones who are involved, many are from broken homes, from parents who drink (of course, they call it social drinking), and from parents who give no thought to raising their children. I attend a small school. I realize that drugs and alcohol problems are probably worse in larger schools, but I still feel there are many good teens who stand up for what is right!" (Female, 17, Mississippi).

"Drugs are pretty common at school, if you ask the right people" (Male, 16, Colorado).

"It's not as bad as everyone else says it is. I haven't ever been asked to do or buy drugs at school. You don't see very many people doing drugs in the school" (Male, 14, Missouri).

"I live in a small town in Minnesota, and I always thought that because of that, drugs and alcohol wouldn't be as bad. But I almost feel that drug and alcohol use is as bad here as it is in the big city" (Female, 15, Minnesota).

"I know in my school I am in a minority of those who don't use drugs or alcohol. A lot of my friends drink. When I go home from a game I wonder how many will live to see the next day. I think people need to realize that there is a large problem and something needs to be done about it. It cannot continue to grow like it has. I hope people will start to realize the danger and the harm that it causes others" (Female, 17, Washington).

What Do We Discover?

What do we learn through such quotes? Many teens use drugs and drink alcohol; many do not. Not too profound, but important just the same. Many teens, like the girl from Texas quoted above, want it known that they don't use drugs. For instance, a 1986 Gallup statistic tells us that 24 percent of the nation's teenagers have smoked marijuana at least once in their lives. But what about the 76 percent who have *never* smoked the drug? They have a voice and an opinion too, but all too often it seems to be lost in the media attention on the drug situation.

With alcohol, abuse is more widespread. Close to one-half of the teens who responded to a *Campus Life* survey question indicated that they drink on a regular basis. Even so, that means that close to one-half are not consuming alcohol. Here are a few comments from the often neglected other half:

"I don't drink or do drugs and I'm glad that I'm responsible enough not to get involved" (Female, 16, California).

"I don't drink because I feel that alcohol is the most widely used and widely accepted drug in this country. But it's still a drug—[it's] just in a different package" (Male, 17, Nevada).

"Using drugs and alcohol doesn't make a party any better. I know! I go to a lot of parties and stay sober and have just as much fun as the drinkers do. Maybe even more" (Female, 15, Michigan).

"I don't need to drink. Even if I would just drink on a 'social' level, the temptation would be there to overuse" (Male, 16, Illinois).

WHY DO USERS USE?

While it's true that there are many viewpoints and that schools vary from community to community, most of the teens I talked to and surveyed admitted that drug abuse takes place in their schools. And in fact many students—possibly ten out of every hundred—are regularly using illegal drugs. Why?

"To wade through the hardness of growing up" (Female, 16, California).

"To be cool and to get a high feeling" (Male, 17, Wisconsin).

"Because I want to lose myself" (Female, 16, Illinois).

"Peer pressure. Pressures from school, home, students" (Male, 17, South Dakota).

"Teenagers use drugs for various reasons. For many, drugs free them from reality and ease their insecurities. Unfortunately, the reality of drugs gives the opposite effect. Others use them to rebel against their parents" (Female, 17, Washington).

"Some use them to get away from their problems, others for experimentation, and most because of peer pressure" (Male, 17, Texas).

"Problems at home, school, friends, problems with themselves" (Female, 17, Texas).

"Peer pressure" (Male, 18, Ohio).

"Kids growing up today are so used to seeing violence, abortions, drugs, drug addicts, alcoholics, that we think it's all right to use drugs and alcohol and have sex before we even get out of school. Most teenagers try at least one of these things before they turn eighteen. And some of us even do things we know are wrong, but we do them anyway" (Female, 18, Michigan).

"To put it all in a nutshell, I used drugs to escape from problems because I never constructively learned how to deal with them. From day one of use, which was when I was around thirteen or fourteen years old, I would drown out any responsibilities or problems with drugs. My getting off of drugs was actually the learning of how to deal with problems for myself. I go to AA meetings and I vent myself and I say, 'Help, I don't know what's going on'" (Male, 18, Chicago).

"A lot of jocks are on speed just to win a game" (Female, 15, Missouri).

"It may sound like a cliché, but I really do have everything in control. Some days I just want to get away, and drugs help" (Female, 17, South Carolina).

"So they don't have to face tests and schoolwork. To escape the real world and try to make life a little funnier and a little easier" (Female, 16, Missouri).

"To make me stronger" (Male, 18, Georgia).

"It makes screwing a chick or dude a lot more fun, and makes it last longer" (Male, 17, Texas).

"Some kids do drugs because they want attention from their parents" (Female, 17, Missouri).

"To fit in with everyone else at parties and stuff. Just to get through school" (Male, 17, Colorado).

"Teenagers go through a lot of stress, and drugs help them forget about their problems—for a little while anyway—and have fun" (Female, 16, Wisconsin).

"To escape reality. The strain on teenagers in today's society is beyond what anyone ever expected" (Male, 18, Arizona).

"I did it because I was curious. I was also sick of monotonous weekends" (Female, 17, California).

"To try something new and escape something old. It's sad that teens feel the world is so bad that the only way to enjoy it is to forget it" (Female, 16, Ohio).

"I don't want to be called a druggie. But do you know how hard it is to be at a party where your friends are passing around a joint, and they pass it to you and you're supposed to say no? It's very hard. In fact, I've never said no! But I really want to" (Female, 14, Florida).

"Our friends want us to try it, and we think they aren't going to tell us to do something that is going to harm us. So we try it" (Male, 16, California).

"Because they are stupid" (Female, 15, Texas).

"To experiment" (Female, 16, New York).

"To have a good time" (Male, 16, Georgia).

"To act older. To go out with the crowd" (Male, 18, Texas).

"Most teenagers use drugs because they have trouble getting along with people and themselves. Also it depends on what kind of neighborhood they live in" (Male, 14, Wisconsin).

"I think teenagers use drugs to feel good and to give them a boost" (Female, 14, Missouri).

"I did them because everyone else was doing them. I also wanted to get my mother mad" (Female, 15, California).

"Because it's fun getting a buzz" (Male, 16, Michigan).

"Because they like to get crazy" (Female, 18, Texas).

"Because they are stupid" (Female, 17, Ohio).

"Problems at home or school" (Female, South Dakota).

"I like the way they make me feel" (Female, 17, Tennessee).

"Because it's something you're not supposed to do" (Male, 15, New York).

"To show off! To show their friends they can do it" (Female, 17, Texas).

"I had a lot of trouble at home because my dad is an alcoholic. He's been through treatment. So I did drugs and alcohol to get rid of problems. Then my dad got straight, but instead of quitting I just kept on using because I still had those feelings inside. I created conflict at home so that I would have a reason to do drugs. After a while the problems will go away, but you have it in your head that the problems are still there just so you can have that reason to use" (Male, 16, Tennessee).

"In the sixties lots of people used drugs and associated them with the psychedelic music they listened to. Psychedelic drugs (acid, PCP) are very bad, but people should try them at least once. Seeing different shades or shapes and different textures is really cool. Hearing things like desks and walls and flowers is fun and so is seeing music. Drugs can be really fun. If someone uses them occasionally, I think it's OK" (Male, 16, South Carolina).

"Because it relaxes them" (Male, 14, Washington).

"Probably to relieve some pressure for a while, to live in a fantasy world where everything is perfect" (Female, 16, Ohio).

"Fun" (Male, 17, South Dakota).

"So many teenagers drink and take drugs because it's like an escape; they go into their own little world and make it what they want it to be. Others take drugs and drink to try to fit in. But I do it because I don't like my life or myself very much, but I don't know how to change it. I know drugs are stupid, but if adults would really listen like they say they will and not lecture as much but explain a bit more, then fewer teenagers would be taking drugs and drinking" (Female, 15, Tennessee).

"Because I like the image, and I just do because that's my choice" (Female, 16, West Virginia).

"I've tried drugs and alcohol because of the pressure, but I never felt anything but guilt and headaches. It's not worth the risk" (Female, 15, New Jersey).

"To get high and express their true feelings" (Female, 16, South Dakota).

"Because they want to freak out" (Male, 16, Texas).

"The high" (Male, 17, Ohio).

"For the effect" (Female, 16, South Dakota).

"To relieve problems, stress, anxiety, and boredom. People keep on using to alleviate the problems that the drugs later cause, so they become addicted" (Male, 15, West Virginia).

"Because the world sucks. I'm young and I only use 15 percent of my brain anyway" (Male, 16, Tennessee).

"I use marijuana because it is a fun drug and it is perfectly harmless physically. The only reason people say not to use pot is because it is illegal. Big deal! It is not harmful unless it is used in an unsafe situation" (Male, 17, South Carolina).

"I used once for the h—— of it" (Male, 15, Illinois).

"Maybe because they feel empty inside and they want something to fill the void" (Female, 17, South Dakota).

"To go along with the crowd" (Male, 17, Georgia).

"Because it's my choice" (Female, 17, Washington).

"I guess I used out of curiosity" (Female, 17, South Carolina).

"Popularity, to make them more outgoing, peer pressure" (Female, 17, Ohio).

"I would have a lot of problems interacting with peers or my family, and I started taking speed and getting drunk so I could become this strong person that everybody likes. I appeared to be real outgoing—my drug use covered up the real person who was hurting. I just didn't want to get rejected anymore. I was being picked on in junior high by kids because I hung out with older kids. So I just wanted to escape from everything" (Female, 18, Illinois).

"Drugs are stupid and the only reason most high school students use them is because they want to be cool. They think it's the cool thing to do" (Female, 15, South Carolina).

"It's like sex. Once you try it, you're hooked" (Male, 17, Michigan).

GRAPH 2 **WHY TEENS WHO HAVE USED SAY THEY USED DRUGS**

If you have used drugs, tell why.

To Experiment/Curiosity   50%   100%
42%

Peer Pressure
23%

To Escape
15%

To Rebel
10%

Feels Good
13%

For Fun
10%

To Relax
4%

Because Drugs Are There
4%

Source: The 1986 *CAMPUS LIFE* survey of high school students. Includes multiple answers.

Experimentation: Giving Way to Other Reasons

The main reason offered for using drugs or alcohol—experimentation—is certainly not surprising. Experimentation is a part of life and essential for personal growth. It plays itself out in normal and often harmless ways: unusual hairdos, new clothing styles, shooting the rapids in a rubber raft, rappelling from a cliff. Yet for the person who uses drugs, experimentation is complicated by many other factors, most of which are not always recognizable at first glance:

The influence of family. While it may not be apparent to most people, adolescent use of alcohol or drugs is often the result of a parent's own use. Most of the former addicts I talked to came from families where substance abuse was present. And while many of these people said they first used "out of curiosity," their long-term abuse and eventual addiction was, they said, attributable to family drug and/or alcohol abuse. According to the Illinois Department of Alcohol and Substance Abuse, 85 to 90 percent of teenage patients in treatment in the Chicago area come from families with drug and alcohol abuse histories. While the national average of 65 percent is lower, it still proves the powerful influence that family drug and alcohol abuse has on teenagers.

Peer pressure. The influence of friends was the number two reason why users said they use. Other studies would rank peer pressure as the number one reason. A study of 350 eleventh- and twelfth-graders by psychologist Fred Beauvis of Colorado State University demonstrates that drug-using friends have a greater influence on teenage drug use than other factors. Beauvis has said, "Once [teenagers] start using drugs, you can do individual therapy, you can involve family and get some good results. But if the kid goes back to the same friends, chances are it won't work."

Low self-worth. Teenagers often continue beyond first-time use because their drug-using friends allow them to feel they belong, no matter how tenuous that belonging may be. The overpowering need to belong is tied very closely to a lack of self-confidence and self-acceptance. One striking example for me was Anita (who is interviewed along with her mother in chapter 6). Her self-concept was so low and her need for love and friends was so great that she turned to drug and alcohol abuse to solve her problems. Yet by turning to substance abuse she only compounded those problems, alienated positive peers, and found herself addicted and suicidal.

I should say that one seventeen-year-old user from Iowa wrote to tell me he believes this is a wrong perception: "I smoke weed myself. You probably think I'm a long-haired druggie. But I'm a three-year varsity letterman, a 3.0 student, and a pretty clean-cut kid. . . . So anyone who thinks people who smoke weed are losers, think again." Another teen user wrote: "I've been accepted to the college of my choice and do fine in school. Why do people try to tell us we have a problem?" Whether or not this guy is really a "winner" is hard to tell from just a short comment. Of the thousands of surveys and letters I read, very few (less than a dozen) expressed his viewpoint. But one important point these two students do make is that drug use cuts across all cliques and peer groups, gaining acceptance by so-called winners *and* so-called losers.

Escape. A seventeen-year-old girl from Washington said: "I feel teen-agers use drugs as an escape. People have made the world so advanced and complex that it is hard for some to fit in." Considering the growing numbers of teens who attempt to "escape" through suicide, I am not surprised that many students gave this reason for their abuse. Many are driven to find an escape because the pressure to perform and excel becomes incredibly stressful. All of this becomes accentuated by the hope-less feelings that often are created by living in a world where the front-page news offers only bad news. It's like knowing there's a time bomb in the school basement, but that there's still that history test to finish. To many teens, that's about as much sense as the world makes. So why not get high and avoid the hassles?

Addiction. No one except former addicts gave me this as a reason for abuse. Long-term abusers do not want to admit dependence because of-ten their abuse began as a fight for independence. It would be one more blow to self-esteem to admit the substance had taken away the control they had fought so long to gain.

No one good reason. Sometimes I hate categories. It would be very easy to choose one of the above factors and attempt to fit each abuser in his or her appropriate place. Yet if my interaction with drug abusers tells me anything, it's that no one reason leads to long-term abuse or addic-tion. To help the abuser, we must work with the total person and all the factors that play into that individual's abuse.

WHAT DO USERS USE?

GRAPH 3 **TOP THREE DRUGS AMONG HIGH SCHOOL STUDENTS**

If you have used drugs, which drugs do you like the most?

Marijuana	50%	100%

88%

Speed/Crank

17%

Cocaine/Crack

16%

(Percentages are of those who have used drugs and include multiple responses.)

Source: The 1986 *CAMPUS LIFE* survey of high school students. Includes multiple answers.

When the general high school population is asked what the most pop-ular drug on campus is, many state that they simply don't know because they avoid that scene altogether. Others, many of whom are users or one-time users, offer this rundown of which drugs are the most popular in their communities:

"Marijuana, because nobody has the money for heavy drugs" (Male, 15, Iowa).

"Reefer [marijuana] is so easy to get and it is a relatively cheap high" (Male, 17, Georgia).

"Marijuana—it's cheap and it won't kill your brain" (Male, 15, Arizona).

"Uppers. Speed. It helps people cope with school life and family problems" (Male, 17, Arizona).

"Pot makes you feel good" (Female, 18, Washington).

"Acid, marijuana, cocaine. They make you feel free" (Male, 14, Arizona).

"Marijuana, because it's cool" (Male, 17, Washington).

"Pot [couldn't be found], so everyone started doing acid" (Female, 16, Arizona).

"The reason kids started using crack and stuff is because cops busted all the major pot dealers. Give us the pot back and we won't do crack and crank" (Female, 15, Illinois).

"Pot, speed, cocaine. They all get you high, relieve the pressure, get you through the day" (Female, 16, Washington).

Marijuana: The Main Drug[1]

Marijuana—often called dope and sometimes referred to as grass, reefer, and Mary Jane—clearly is the drug most users prefer. Most heavy dope smokers would push for legalization because they feel, contrary to information coming out of the National Institute on Drug Abuse, that "it's not really a dangerous drug." Here are some basic facts about this popular drug:

What is it? Marijuana "joints" or cigarettes are made from the dried particles of the *Cannabis sativa* plant. The mind-altering ingredient in marijuana is THC (delta-9-tetrahydrocannabinol), but there are more than four hundred other chemicals in the plant. The amount of THC determines how strong the drug's effects will be. Due to increasing sophistication in growing techniques, today's marijuana is ten times greater in THC strength than the marijuana used in the early 1970s. This more potent marijuana increases the physical and mental effects and the possibility of health problems in the abuser.

---

[1]Most of the information on the effects of marijuana, amphetamines, and LSD was excerpted or adapted from material published by the National Institute on Drug Abuse/Department of Health and Human Services.

Hashish. Hashish or hash is a "highly refined" drug derived from the resin of the leaves and flowers of the marijuana plant. It is usually much stronger than crude marijuana, containing five to ten times more THC. The substances sold on the street as THC often turn out to be something else, like PCP (an hallucinogen).

Physical effects. The effects of marijuana use vary from user to user and may include feelings of euphoria, relaxed inhibitions, increased appetite, disorientation, eventual fatigue, lack of coordination, poor short-term memory. The drug may act as a stimulant, depressant, or hallucinogen. Also, marijuana use can negatively affect:

- Driving skills. Because marijuana affects a wide range of coordination and mental skills, it greatly impairs the ability to drive and run machinery safely.
- Heart and lungs. Marijuana increases the heart rate and can cause chest pains in people with a poor blood supply to the heart. Marijuana can be especially harmful to the lungs because users inhale the unfiltered smoke deeply and hold it in their lungs as long as possible. Since the smoke has such long contact with lung tissue it increases the possibility of damage. Marijuana smoke contains some of the ingredients that cause emphysema and lung cancer.
- Pregnancy. Some research indicates that marijuana use during pregnancy may cause premature births and low birth weights. Studies of men and women who use marijuana have shown that the drug may influence levels of some hormones relating to sexuality. Women may have irregular menstrual cycles, and both men and women may have a temporary loss of fertility. Because the teenage years are a time of rapid physical and sexual development, these findings suggest that marijuana use during those years may be especially harmful to long-term development.

Acute panic/anxiety reaction. A common negative reaction to marijuana is the "acute panic/anxiety reaction." In describing this reaction, users say it's an extreme fear of losing control, thus the reason for panic. This reaction usually disappears in a few hours.

Psychological dependence. Long-term users may become psychologically dependent on the drugs. Users may have a hard time limiting their use, and they may have to increase the amount of drug used to get similar effects to what they had during early use. As in any dependence, use begins to affect relationships, studies, job responsibilities, and other aspects of the users' lives.

A gateway drug. One of drug experts' growing concerns is that marijuana serves as a gateway to the use of harder drugs. One nineteen-year-
old former user from Colorado told me, "You may start on something
really light, like marijuana, and you get burned out by that, so someone
else hands you something different, something a little stronger—and
you go on and on from there. A lot of people get bored with one thing
and go on to something heavier, and that's what leads people to be on cocaine and heroin, the heavy stuff. I've seen a lot of that happen."

Uppers
Coming in at a not-very-close second to marijuana as most popular
among drug users are various forms of uppers or stimulants. The drugs
that are named most frequently in this category are speed (a tablet, pill,
or capsule often called ups and black beauties) and crank (often found in
the form of white powder, but sold in tablets, pills, or "rock" form, and
sometimes called crystal, crystal meth, and methedrine). What's confusing about these two types of stimulants is that they are both sometimes referred to as "speed." Both are stimulants and both have similar
effects on the user. For the sake of convenience I will discuss them
together:

What are they? Stimulants or uppers refer to several groups of drugs
that tend to increase alertness and physical activity. Some people use
stimulants to counteract drowsiness or "down" feelings caused by sleeping pills or alcohol. This up/down cycle is extremely dangerous and hard
on the body. Along with amphetamines (speed), drug literature typically
includes cocaine and caffeine in its list of stimulants.

Medical use. Amphetamines are used to treat narcolepsy (a rare disor-
der marked by uncontrolled sleep episodes), and minimal brain dysfunc-
tion (MBI) in children. They also are prescribed for short-term treatment
of obesity.

Physical effects. These drugs increase heart and breathing rates, increase blood pressure, dilate pupils, and decrease appetite. In addition,
they can cause a dry mouth, sweating, headaches, blurred vision, dizziness, sleeplessness, and anxiety. Extremely high doses can cause people
to flush or become pale. Amphetamines can cause a rapid or irregular
heartbeat, tremors, loss of coordination, and even physical collapse. An
amphetamine injection creates a sudden increase in blood pressure that
can cause death from stroke, very high fever, or heart failure.

The high. Users say they experience restlessness, anxiety, and moodi-
ness. Higher doses intensify the effects and the user can become excited

and talkative and feel a false sense of self-confidence and power. People who use large amounts of amphetamines over a long period of time also can develop an amphetamine psychosis, which results in hallucinations (seeing, hearing, and feeling things that do not exist) and in paranoia (the feeling that others are out to get them). People in this extremely suspicious state frequently exhibit bizarre and sometimes violent behavior. These symptoms usually disappear when use is stopped.

The long-term effects. Long-term use of amphetamines can lead to malnutrition, skin disorders, ulcers, and various diseases that come with vitamin deficiencies. Lack of sleep, weight loss, and depression also result from regular use. Frequent use of large amounts of amphetamines can produce brain damage resulting in speech and thought disturbances. Injecting amphetamines intravenously can cause various infections, including AIDS (from using nonsterile needles), serious infections (from self-prepared, contaminated solutions of the drug), kidney damage, strokes, tissue damage, lung or heart disease, and other possibly fatal diseases of the blood vessels.

Dependence. Some users report a psychological dependence, a feeling that the drug is essential to keeping a normal grip on life. These users frequently continue to use amphetamines to avoid the "down" mood they get when the drug wears off. People who use amphetamines regularly may also develop "tolerance," the need to take larger doses to get the same first-time effect. When people suddenly stop using the drug, they may experience fatigue, long periods of sleep, irritability, hunger, and depression. The length and severity of the depression seems related to how much and how often amphetamines were used.

Cocaine: The "Glamour" Drug
Cocaine and its highly potent, smokable form, crack, are other popular drugs, despite the growing research proving cocaine's dangerous, highly addictive, and sometimes lethal effects. An eighteen-year-old girl from the suburbs of Chicago told how she first started "doing lines" or "snorting" cocaine:

"Mainly I used to just smoke pot. . . . I started hanging around with a bunch of people from Chicago, and one day they asked me if I wanted to drop off some cocaine to someone else; they had given me some money and I said fine. So I brought it over to this house downtown (I was thirteen at the time), and they asked me if I wanted to do a couple of lines and I said sure. So I did it and I was just fascinated. I was really interested in the drug because I had never done it before. It made me feel older and real alive and like I could do anything. I kept using it for three or four months and I ended up having a lot of sinus problems and my nose was bleeding a lot."

Along with some of the physical symptoms of snorting, such as frequent nose bleeds, users and ex-users often mention a feeling of euphoria, the belief that you can do almost anything while on the drug. An eighteen-year-old guy from Chicago described it this way: "It sped me out, you know. My internals, I mean, I could feel that my internals were just pumping a lot faster and I felt like I had the ability to do so much more. I had so much energy. This one time I went home and made french fries, I cleaned the whole kitchen, I was just laughing at everything. You think you have so much power. But you are really clumsy— the kitchen really turned into a mess. I would feel that craziness high of it, that power trip—[that feeling] that you could conquer anything."

Cocaine users may also feel calm, as though nothing can upset them. One nineteen-year-old girl from Colorado describes it this way: "I was drunk this one night. I didn't want to go home drunk, so I took a line and it burned my nostrils so bad for a while, and then it made me feel like nothing's wrong. Coke puts you at ease. You can deal with anything when you're on coke. My mom and dad were upset with me when I got home but I could deal with it. I wasn't mad, I was happy. It lasted about three hours, because it was my first time, otherwise it wouldn't have lasted that long. I think that's why cocaine is one of the most used drugs because it makes you feel like there's nothing wrong in the world."

Another sixteen-year-old girl, also from the suburbs of Chicago, describes her cocaine use a bit differently: "I didn't like cocaine. I only liked the way it felt when it went up my nose and that was it. I didn't like the high I got off it at all. It made me paranoid; my nose got cold and my palms got sweaty. I didn't know where I was going or what I was doing. I didn't like the high at all. That's why I didn't do it very much. Cocaine is the glamour drug and I did it basically to be cool. I liked the feeling of doing it, but I didn't like the high."

Coke is unpredictable, and each user reacts differently. A seventeen-year-old guy from Illinois said: "Cocaine speeds you up. I really didn't want to be up. The drug made me itchy and nervous and all ready to go, and I didn't want to feel like that."

For some, as recent news reports tell us, the first use may be the last. A seventeen-year-old guy from rural Tennessee explained: "I did some crack just once and it scared me. I thought I was going to die. I don't want to talk about it." I can still remember how this person, a struggling former drug user, became watery-eyed and trembled even at the mention of cocaine. To him it was far from a glamour drug.

So what is cocaine really? Here are some facts:

What is it? Cocaine is extracted from the leaves of South America's coca trees. Like amphetamines, or speed, it is a central-nervous-system stimulant. Cocaine appears in several different forms. The most available form is cocaine hydrochloride, usually a fine, white, crystal-like powder used medically as a local anesthetic. On the street, however, it may come in larger pieces or "rocks."

Method of Use. Cocaine is usually sniffed or snorted into the nose (this is often referred to as "doing lines" or "lining"). Some users inject it or smoke freebase, another form of the drug.

Immediate effects. When snorting or "lining" cocaine, the effects begin within fifteen or twenty minutes and disappear in an hour. Effects include dilated pupils and increased blood pressure, heart and breathing rates, and body temperature. The user may have a sense of well-being, feel more energetic or alert, and be less hungry. However, reactions and effects vary widely from user to user.

Effects of freebasing. Smoking freebase produces a shorter and more intense high than most other ways of using, because smoking is the most direct and rapid way to get the drug to the brain. Since large amounts are getting to the brain more rapidly, smoking also increases the risks associated with cocaine. These risks include confusion, slurred speech, anxiety, and serious psychological problems.

Overall effects. The dangers of cocaine vary from user to user, depending on the dosage and how the drug is taken. Some regular users talk about feelings of restlessness, irritability, anxiety, and sleeplessness. In some people, even low doses create psychological problems. People who use high doses over a long period of time many become paranoid or experience what is called "cocaine psychosis," which may include hallucinations.

Physical dangers. Occasional use can cause a stuffy or runny nose, while long-term lining can ulcerate the mucous membrane of the nose. Injecting cocaine with unsterile equipment can cause hepatitis or other infections (including AIDS). Furthermore, because preparation of freebase involves the use of chemically volatile solvents, deaths and serious injuries from fire or explosions can occur (as was the situation with comedian Richard Pryor). Overdose deaths can occur when the drug is injected, smoked, or even snorted (which happened to basketball hopeful Len Bias after his first and only use). Deaths are caused by multiple seizures that are followed by respiratory and cardiac arrest.

Addiction. By now most of us have seen commercials or heard reports about the lab monkey who gave up eating, drinking, and sex for more cocaine. Sometimes people continue use just to avoid the depression and fatigue they would feel if they stopped. Overall, cocaine is highly addictive and demanding; it has caused users to abandon friends, family, hopes, and dreams to continue in their use of the drug.

LSD: A Sixties Revival?

I was surprised at the number of students who talk about the popularity and relative cheapness of that psychedelic of the sixties, LSD. For around $2.50, the drug can be purchased in "dot" form (the substance is "blotted" on a thin square of paper and swallowed). One nineteen-year-old girl from Michigan told me she saw "elephants in the school hallway" after taking the substance.

A sixteen-year-old girl from Colorado related the fear of nightmarish flashbacks: "I haven't done acid for over a year. About two months after I quit doing acid, I started hallucinating again. I haven't had a relapse since, but it's possible. It scares you to know that the acid can come back and give you a bad trip, that you could go on a trip that you would never get off. The acid is still in my system."

Some facts about LSD and other hallucinogens:

What are hallucinogens? Hallucinogens or psychedelics are drugs that affect the user's perceptions, sensations, thinking, self-awareness, and emotions. Hallucinogens include LSD, mescaline, psilocybin (mushrooms), and DMT. Some hallucinogens come from natural sources—mescaline, for example, is derived from the peyote cactus. Others are synthetic or manufactured.

What is LSD? LSD is manufactured from lysergic acid, which is found in the ergot fungus that grows in rye and other grains. LSD was discovered in 1938 and is one of the most potent mood-changing chemicals around. It is odorless, colorless, and tasteless, and is sold on the street in tablets, capsules, or liquid form. It usually is taken by mouth, but it can be injected. Often it is added to absorbent paper, such as blotter paper, and divided into small decorated squares. Each square (often called a dot) is one dose.

Effects. The effects of psychedelics are unpredictable and depend on the amount taken, the user's personality, mood, and expectations, and the surroundings in which the drug is used. Usually, the user feels the first effects of the drug thirty to ninety minutes after taking it. The physical effects include dilated pupils, higher body temperature, increased heart rate and blood pressure, sweating, loss of appetite, sleeplessness, dry mouth, and tremors.

Sensations and feelings change too. The user may feel many different emotions at once or swing rapidly from one emotion to another. The person's sense of time and self change. Sensations may seem to collide, giving the user the feeling of "hearing" colors and "seeing" sounds. While some users talk about the enjoyment they get out of such "crossover" experiences, many find them frightening and may panic as a result.

Bad trips. Having a bad psychological reaction to LSD and similar drugs is common. The scary sensations may last anywhere from a few minutes to several hours and be mildly frightening or completely terrifying. The user may experience panic, confusion, suspiciousness, anxiety, and feelings of helplessness or loss of control. Sometimes taking a hallucinogen such as LSD can unmask emotional problems that were previously unknown to the user. Flashbacks, in which the person experiences a drug's effects without having to take the drug again, can occur at any time.

Effects of heavy use. Research has shown some changes in the mental abilities of heavy LSD users, but those changes are not present in all cases. Heavy users sometimes develop signs of brain damage, such as impaired memory and attention span, mental confusion, and difficulty with abstract thinking. These signs may be subtle. It is not yet known whether such mental changes are permanent or if they disappear when LSD use is stopped.

What's Left?

Of course, there are dozens of other drugs, such as "ecstasy" or XTC (one of the so-called "designer" drugs), white crosses (a combination of speed and marijuana), mushroom or rooms (psilocybin, a hallucinogen) and Valium (a depressant). While there isn't enough space to analyze all of these, you will find more information on various categories of drugs in Appendix One.

However, we do need to mention a few drugs that most people don't think of as drugs. First, cigarettes. Many of the students who participated in surveys and interviews identified cigarettes as a type of drug. (The National Institute on Drug Abuse draws some striking comparisons between the use of and dependence on nicotine and dependence on illegal drugs.) Caffeine tablets such as *Nodoz* are attractive to some users because they are cheap, easy to obtain, and legal. And many insist that alcohol fits in the drug category.

Steroids were mentioned only occasionally on the *Campus Life* survey, which may have been because the use of steroids generally is limited to a select group of jocks or aspiring jocks. Though steroids are not a typical "get high" kind of substance, they do increase the body's natural production of the male hormone testosterone and thus can increase body and muscle size. However, like regular street drugs, steroids are said to have addictive qualities. Also, according to the experts, steroids may have some rather traumatic effects, such as hair loss, uncontrolled aggression, an increased chance of heart disease (as early as age thirty), and the development of milk-producing breasts by teenage males.

RESPONSIBLE DRUG USE?

GRAPH 4
IS THERE SUCH A THING AS RESPONSIBLE DRUG USE?

NO (with the exception of "prescriptions or medical reasons only")

	50%	100%

82%

YES, Recreational

17%

OTHER

1%

(Percentages are of all high school students surveyed.)

Source: The 1986 *CAMPUS LIFE* survey of high school students.

In the *Campus Life* survey, close to two out of ten teens felt there is such a thing as a responsible use of street drugs. These individuals primarily advise "Don't overdo it." This number of respondents is in line with the 19 percent who, on another *Campus Life* survey question, stated that drug use should not be against the law. (Both percentages are higher than the 10 percent who claim to be currently using. This could be because some students who are not currently using still feel use is OK, or because some nonusers take a "live and let live" attitude toward life.)

To the people in this group, responsible use is described in the following ways:

"If you don't become addicted and if you can handle it" (Female, 16, California).

"I think you yourself have the ability to take on a responsibility maturely. That is, you should be able to do anything you want. [Using] drugs is just one aspect and something that people take too seriously. If you screw up your life, it is nobody's fault but your own" (Female, 18, Ohio).

"Depends on the person" (Male, 18, Wisconsin).

"When I drive I don't smoke marijuana" (Male, 17, Iowa).

"To the point before overdose" (Male, 18, Wisconsin).

"Do drugs only in your own home" (Male, 17, Arizona).

"I think 'soft drugs' like marijuana and speed are less dangerous, have less side effects, and should be considered legal drugs. 'Harder' substances such as cocaine and heroin are too dangerous and could affect public health and should be considered illegal" (Male, 16, South Dakota).

"I think it's OK to use speed to help you stay awake at work" (Female, 14, Wisconsin).

Now for the Other Side

For the most part, however, the teenagers surveyed feel the only responsible use of drugs is for medical purposes, as prescribed by a doctor. Some typical answers refuting the idea of a responsible use of street drugs include:

"Drug users are not fooling anyone except themselves. They think that they are cool and that they can handle it, but they can't. They just can't" (Female, 15, Illinois).

"Drugs can create more problems. And it's stupid" (Male, 16, Georgia).

"I feel drugs can hurt me and my pursuit of a career in sports" (Male, 16, Tennessee).

"Because [smoked substance] destroys your lungs" (Male, 15, Illinois).

"People who do drugs are a hazard to the rest of this community, not only to themselves" (Female, 15, Texas).

"Drug use is not only dangerous to the health of the user, but it also hurts others around him, including family and friends" (Female, 16, Washington).

"Drug use goes against my set of morals. I feel that anyone who uses drugs proves they are weak by trying to make themselves pseudo-strong. I'm mentally strong enough to realize I have weaknesses and must deal with them in other ways besides drugs" (Male, 18, South Carolina).

"Drugs are dangerous and not worth blowing your money over; they only start an ugly habit" (Male, 17, South Carolina).

"I am an athlete and I don't need drugs to screw me up. I'm scared to use them anyway, because you could die. You never know what's in those things. After Len Bias's experience, I don't want to ever touch [drugs]" (Female, 15, Illinois).

"My advice to anyone who is thinking of using drugs to gain popularity, or for any other reason, is not to do it! Drugs can destroy your whole future" (Female, 14, Texas).

"I have no need to take drugs. They don't help you at all. They restrict the things that you are able to do" (Male, 15, Illinois).

"I stopped using because I found out I was killing myself" (Female, 17, Georgia).

"My brother had been on drugs, mainly acid, for three years, and he went crazy" (Female, 17, Idaho).

"People who take drugs should open their eyes and see what they are doing to themselves" (Male, 15, Illinois).

"Drugs are not worth all the consequences" (Male, 16, Illinois).

"Drugs aren't something to play around with. I stopped using because I saw that if I didn't quit it could mess me up or I could get addicted to them. And I was taught not to use drugs" (Male, 18, Georgia).

"Drugs suck" (Male, 16, California).

"It seems a terrible way to waste your time, money, and brain" (Female, 15, West Virginia).

"I don't need to get high. I feel good already" (Male, 15, South Carolina).

"My body is a gift, and I don't want to destroy physical abilities that some people don't have" (Female, 17, Illinois).

"I think drugs are stupid, everything from weed to cocaine. Two years ago I used to smoke weed, then I found out I have a natural high. I don't need something to do it for me, so I stopped doing weed, just like that" (Female, 17, Texas).

"Drugs f—— up your brain and body" (Male, 17, Nevada).

"Anybody who uses drugs is an immature person" (Male, 15, South Carolina).

"Drugs can kill you" (Male, 14, West Virginia).

"I have never used drugs. I look at drug use like I look at being a virgin: Once you've done it, you can never say you haven't" (Male, 17, South Carolina).

"I stopped using drugs because I didn't want to be with druggies; I didn't need drugs" (Female, 15, Illinois).

"Drugs will make your children deformed" (Female, 14, West Virginia).

"I don't use because I am afraid of becoming addicted, and when people are on drugs they have less control over a situation" (Female, 15, South Carolina).

GRAPH 5 **KEEP DRUGS AGAINST THE LAW**

Should it be against the law to use drugs?

YES   50%   100%
                                        77%
NO
         19%
Other/No Response
  4%

Source: The 1986 *CAMPUS LIFE* survey of high school students.

More than three out of four students surveyed say that drug use should definitely be against the law. This figure compares closely with the number of students who have never used illegal drugs. There appears to be a feeling that, as feeble as the laws are, they are better than no laws at all.

Some Time for Reflection
In view of the many proven and possible negative effects of drug abuse, it would seem that those who believe in "responsible drug use" either remain very much in the dark about the consequences and hazards of drug abuse, or they want to keep using despite the evidence against it.

Again, teenagers turn to drug use for a variety of complex reasons. While we may be turned off at the user's belligerent attitude when he says things like, "Use to the point of overdose," we must try to see beyond those remarks to the hurting individual within. Simply writing such people off with labels like "druggie," "stoner," and "burnout," feeds harmful stereotypes and further degrades an already fragile personality.

Even more than this, we must seek to be consistent in our attitudes. In the next chapter, we turn to alcohol use. Many students, like those quoted in the section above, have strong reasons against drug use. Yet many of those same people ignore such reasoning when it comes to America's most prominent drug: alcohol. The next chapter explores the reasons for and results of this inconsistent way of thinking.

TWO

DRINKS FOR EVERYBODY?

When the discussion topic moves from illegal street drugs to alcohol, attitudes shift radically. "I hope I don't sound like a hypocrite," commented a fifteen-year-old guy from Ohio, "but I don't believe alcohol is as addictive and deadly as drugs." Over and over again, those who view the use of street drugs as uncool, stupid, and only for losers see drinking as acceptable:

"I never say yes to anything but alcohol and cigarettes, which I know are drugs themselves, but not as bad. My friends feel the same way I do" (Female, 16, Michigan).

"A fact in my high school and my graduating class, which I think is unbelievable, is that most of our honor students (the top 10 percent) are party animals. All I hear on Monday morning is what a great party I missed" (Female, 17, Illinois).

"I don't need drugs. I do drink for pleasure" (Male, 17, Tennessee).

"I don't need drugs; I like the taste of alcohol and the buzz it gives" (Male, 17, Idaho).

"I have heard too many sad-ending stories involving drugs and I don't want to be involved. . . . I drink because it tastes good and because other people are also drinking" (Female, 16, Idaho).

"Drugs are for dirtballs, drinking is a riot" (Male, 17, Michigan).

"Most people who use drugs are from the lower class. These students don't have anything else to do but smoke their pot to try and rid themselves of their problems. . . . Alcohol is widespread throughout the entire high school and every social class. Students basically drink to have a good time" (Male, 17, Michigan).

"I don't use drugs because I'm already very high on life. . . . I love the taste of wine with certain meals. And I have a taste for beer" (Male, 15, Illinois).

"The alcohol problem seems to be more of a problem than drugs. More people think it is cool to drink—but if you take drugs you'll probably have a scummy reputation" (Female, 15, Missouri).

"Drugs will harm your body. Sometimes I like to drink to help me relax" (Female, 17, West Virginia).

"Teenagers use drugs because they are depressed and lonely. Teenagers drink alcohol to be accepted, because everyone else does" (Female, 15, Ohio).

"Alcohol is not as addictive as drugs. I get drunk to have fun" (Female, 18, Texas).

"I have nothing against drinking. I just don't like drugs" (Female, 16, Michigan).

"I am afraid to do drugs, because I have seen how they've hurt my friends. However, while drinking is a very big problem in my family, it doesn't affect my decisions about drinking very much. I don't really know why" (Female, 17, Missouri).

"Teenagers use drugs because they are idiots. Teenagers drink to forget problems, because it tastes good, and it makes the party" (Female, 17, Minnesota).

"I don't need drugs. I drink to go wild with my friends" (Female, 17, Idaho).

"You aren't doing yourself a favor when you use drugs and you can die. I drink because I like the taste of some alcohol" (Male, 16, Idaho).

"Drugs are bad for the system and they may cause many accidents. . . . I drink when I'm depressed or feeling down; it will get me going again" (Female, 16, Georgia).

"Most of my senior acquaintances are too cool *not* to drink" (Female, 17, Texas).

Labels and Inconsistency
One sixteen-year-old I talked to has this to say about those who drink, yet condemn people who use drugs:

"I'm not sure, really, why teenagers drink. Probably for popularity. Most of the jocks drink. But the problem is they separate people as 'burnouts,' and 'jocks,' and 'middle class.' But the burnouts are people, too. The only reason they are called burnouts is because of the way they dress and maybe because they smoke pot. And most of the jocks do the same exact thing, probably worse, but they dress nice and they are in sports. That's a problem in high school. You label people as soon as you see them."

(The *Campus Life* survey tells us that 44 percent of those surveyed drink with some regularity. This figure includes those who drink daily, on weekends, and once a month.)

GRAPH 6 **HOW OFTEN DO STUDENTS DRINK?**

How often do you drink?

Rarely or Never   50%   100%

56%

At Least Occasionally

44%

When do you drink?

On the Weekends

61.5%

Once a Month

36.5%

Daily

2%

(Percentages are from the 44 percent who say they drink.)

Source: The 1986 *CAMPUS LIFE* survey of high school students.

Age and Drinking

Because the *Campus Life* survey did not break students down by age categories (its figures represent averaged responses of students aged fourteen to eighteen), it missed the fact that teens who don't drink at age fourteen still have a strong likelihood of drinking at age eighteen. The American Public Health Association tells us that at age fourteen, about two out of every five American males and about one out of every five American females drink alcohol at least once a month. By age eighteen, nine out of ten males and eight out of ten females drink alcohol at least once a month. According to those findings, the tendency to use increases as students get older. (The percentages decrease slightly as people move out of adolescence.) Those students who claim at age fourteen that they will never drink often change their minds as they reach the latter part of their teenage years. Younger students opposed to drinking would do themselves a great favor—and possibly be better able to stick to their early convictions—if they educated themselves thoroughly on the potential health and safety hazards associated with alcohol consumption.

GRAPH 7 **PATTERNS OF ALCOHOL USE BY SEX AND AGE**

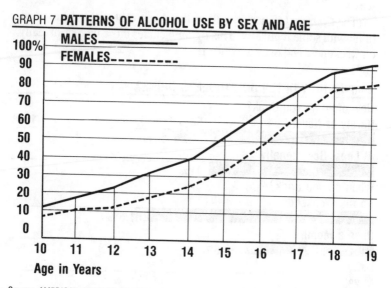

Source: *AMERICAN JOURNAL OF PUBLIC HEALTH* (1984). Used with permission.

Beer: Holding Its Own

In terms of popularity, beer continues to hold its own. Wine, however, is gaining in popularity especially among girls. This increased interest in wine could, of course, have a lot to do with wine cooler ads, which are aimed at the young and the beautiful.

AND THE QUESTION: WHY?

So why do teens drink? Here are some reasons:

"To catch a buzz. That's what most teenagers will tell you. I'm an alcoholic trying to recover. I always liked to 'catch a buzz' too" (Female, 16, Michigan).

"Because California Coolers taste good" (Female, 16, Nevada).

"Sure not for the taste, but to get drunk" (Female, 15, Michigan).

"To get a good feeling and to impress friends" (Male, 14, Ohio).

"For a sense of security" (Female, 17, Texas).

GRAPH 8 **THE MOST POPULAR DRINKS**

What do you drink?

BEER   50%   100%

▰▰▰▰▰▰▰▰▰▰▰▰▰▰▰▰ **Male 69%**
▰▰▰▰▰▰▰▰▰▰▰▰▰▰ **Female 62%**

WINE (includes coolers)

▰▰▰▰▰▰▰▰▰ **Male 40%**
▰▰▰▰▰▰▰▰▰▰ **Female 48%**

HARD LIQUOR

▰▰▰▰▰ **Male 26%**
▰▰▰▰▰ **Female 25%**

(Percentages are from students who say they drink. Includes multiple answers.)

Source: The 1986 *CAMPUS LIFE* survey of high school students.

"Special occasions. Like a sip on New Years' Eve" (Male, 17, Georgia).

"I think drugs and alcohol are abused by teens because they are ignorant and blind to the effects and consequences" (Female, 16, Missouri).

"I think kids in our town drink because basically there is nothing better to do on a Friday or Saturday night" (Female, 15, Missouri).

"The person who feels unaccepted, inadequate, unable to accept himself, feels like drinking because he can gain acceptance through doing it" (Male, 16, Colorado).

"Our society is oriented around alcohol; it's rooted in every crevice of our culture, from the young to the very old" (Male, 16, South Dakota).

"To fit into the crowd; people pay more attention to you when you're drunk" (Male, 14, Washington).

"I drink to talk more freely and to have a good time" (Female, 17, Tennessee).

"When teenagers drink they think they're rebelling against society, but in fact they are conforming to the current culture" (Male, 16, Texas).

"They have a twisted idea of what fun is" (Male, 15, Oregon).

"Your boyfriend or girlfriend is a big influence in getting you into drugs and alcohol" (Female, 16, Colorado).

"Some kids can have everything going for them and they still drink to have fun" (Female, 15, Ohio).

"I enjoy drinking with friends" (Female, 18, Tennessee).

"Seems like the thing to do" (Female, 16, Georgia).

"I think because it's something you are not supposed to do and teenagers think they're getting away with something when they drink. They think they're having a good time and being cool" (Female, 14, Washington).

"I drink because I may be depressed or around people who are drinking" (Female, 17, Georgia).

"To have fun and get trashed" (Male, 16, Ohio).

"Something to do" (Female, 15, Georgia).

"To look grown-up and feel like somebody when you are around others who drink. For the kicks, also" (Female, 17, Wisconsin).

"Because 'everyone else does,' which isn't true" (Female, 15, Ohio).

"Just because it makes a person more carefree. There is really no reason. Just because it's fun getting that relaxed, laughing feeling. I don't think there is too much peer pressure anymore. It's not the main excuse anymore" (Female, 16, Washington).

"I drink because everyone around is drinking too" (Female, 16, West Virginia).

"I feel really relaxed when I drink. I don't drink just to have fun and get drunk. I like it because it makes me relax" (Male, 16, Illinois).

"Teenagers drink alcohol for something to do. To have fun with all your friends. To get drunk!" (Female, 18, Wisconsin).

"Most teenagers drink alcohol for one reason: They think it's fun and because most of their friends do it" (Male, 16, Ohio).

"To go out and party and have a good time" (Female, 15, West Virginia).

"Just for pleasure" (Female, 15, Washington).

"Beer tastes good, but I drink mainly because everybody else drinks" (Male, 15, Illinois).

"To loosen up. Rebellion" (Male, 18, South Dakota).

"Adult influence" (Male, 16, Ohio).

"I drink because I think it makes parties a bit funner, and it's not hard to get, and it's not very expensive" (Male, 16, Illinois).

"Because it makes me more exciting" (Female, 15, West Virginia).

"To be big and be in the in-group, like the jocks" (Male, 16, Michigan).

"Peer pressure, to escape problems, overcome shyness" (Female, 17, Texas).

"I have a glass of wine on the Christmas holiday" (Female, 14, West Virginia).

"To have fun" (Female, 14, Washington).

"I drink because I have a type of craving for it, but not often" (Female, 15, South Carolina).

"I know a lot of people drink because everyone else does. I've noticed that kids will try things and will drink maybe a little bit, then get pressured to do more" (Female, 14, Nevada).

"I guess I drink so that I can get away from school, thoughts, and pressure from my parents. I also happen to like it" (Male, 15, Illinois).

"I drink to get wasted and to feel funky" (Female, 16, Nevada).

"I don't drink to get drunk, just to enjoy myself" (Female, 15, West Virginia).

"I really don't know why I drink" (Male, 17, Illinois).

"There are different reasons for every teenager" (Female, 18, Ohio).

"I drink for the pleasure of drinking, just like I would drink a Coke or Pepsi" (Male, 17, South Carolina).

"There is nothing else to do on the weekends" (Male, 15, Idaho).

"To fit in and feel older. Some also think it's a challenge to break the law" (Female, 18, South Dakota).

"I just drink when I'm around my friends so they won't leave me out and think I'm a drag! But I don't drink to where I put myself or others in danger" (Male, 15, South Carolina).

"Teenagers like alcohol and it doesn't seem harmful to them" (Female, 17, Ohio).

"Drinking makes me f—— rowdy and I love it. You're f—— stupid not to drink" (Male, 17, Illinois).

"Maybe your friends aren't pressuring you, but you feel more secure!" (Female, 14, Michigan).

"Sometimes I get a lot of stuff inside me and I drink my troubles away, or I'll go to a party and drink" (Female, 15, South Carolina).

"To look important" (Female, 14, Texas).

"Mainly for social reasons, but it's also been an escape for me" (Male, 16, California).

"To calm themselves down; maybe they're mad and alcohol makes them relax" (Female, 15, Ohio).

"I only drink on special occasions or to celebrate" (Male, 15, South Carolina).

"Just to drown my sorrows. But they are always there when my head stops spinning" (Female, 16, Georgia).

"Peer pressure" (Female, 16, Texas).

"I feel most teens drink for a common purpose. The fact that it is not approved of by adults only adds to the pleasure of getting away with it" (Female, 15, South Carolina).

"Enjoyment" (Male, 15, Illinois).

"Because everyone else drinks" (Female, 16, West Virginia).

"Because their friends do it and it makes them feel older—not just because they're thirsty" (Male, 17, Wisconsin).

"Because of the macho image portrayed by the TV commercials" (Male, 15, Wisconsin).

"To get drunk and to have a reason for acting the way they do" (Female, 14, Washington).

"I don't think it's necessary for me to drink. I just like to, especially when I'm with my friends" (Female, 15, South Carolina).

"My parents let me" (Male, 15, Illinois).

"Because I'm mad or in a bad mood" (Male, 17, Florida).

"I drink because everybody else is" (Male, 16, Nevada).

"Peer pressure forces me to drink so I won't be a nobody" (Male, 16, Illinois).

"Drinking helps you forget the problems and pressures of the world for a little while" (Female, 18, Texas).

"Status" (Male, 17, Washington).

Peer Pressure: Yes or No?

When talking about the "whys" behind drinking it's important to contrast drinking with the use of illegal or street drugs. Drugs often are seen by teenagers as an escape; many teens look down on drug users. But while students admit that alcohol is a drug, they believe it isn't as bad as illegal or street drugs. As the last person quoted above says, alcohol use is often seen as a symbol of "status."

But what does that mean? Are status, popularity, and being cool just other names for peer pressure? Think about this: When addressed with the more general question, "Why do teenagers say they drink?" the greatest number of teens claim it is due to peer pressure. Then when the question turns personal, "Why do you drink?" just as many say "for fun" as say "because of peer pressure." (Girls, however, are a bit more willing than guys to identify "peer pressure" as their personal reason for drinking.)

Why this difference in motivation when the question turns personal? Considering the negative connotations behind peer pressure, it's not surprising that few teenage drinkers want to claim it as their main reason for drinking (although about one-third still admit that peer pressure motivates them to drink). One sixteen-year-old girl from Washington said: "Teenagers drink because it is fun and very social. I also feel that drugs and alcohol often are blamed on peer pressure. I don't think this is true.

GRAPH 9 WHY TEENS SAY TEENS DRINK

Why do you think teenagers drink alcohol?

Peer Pressure	50%	100%

61%

To Escape
27%

For Fun
24%

Feels Good
17%

To Look More Mature
9%

To Rebel
6%

To Experiment/Curious
5%

Tastes Good
5%

To Relax
5%

Someone in Family Drinks
3%

Ignorant of Bad Effects
2%

Bored
2%

Excitement/Danger
1%

Raise Self-esteem
1%

To Prove I Can Handle It
1%

Advertising
1%

Source: The 1986 *CAMPUS LIFE* survey of high school students. Includes multiple answers.

People are more secure than that. If someone does drink or use drugs because their friends do, it is out of curiosity, not peer pressure."

Many others simply say that blaming peer pressure is a "cop-out," a poor excuse to avoid taking personal responsibility for one's own behav-

GRAPH 10 **WHY TEENS WHO DRINK SAY THEY DRINK**

If you drink, tell why.

	50%	100%

For Fun

Male 37%

Female 33%

Peer Pressure

Male 22%

Female 43%

Because It Tastes Good

Male 10%

Female 20%

To Escape

Male 10%

Female 14%

Because It Feels Good

Male 8%

Female 13%

Because Drinking Relaxes

Male 10%

Female 10%

For Special Occasions Only (Weddings, Christmas, Etc.)

Male 12%

Female 7%

To Rebel

Male 10%

Female 0%

To Experiment/Curious

Male 2%

Female 1%

To Get Drunk

Male 2%

Female 1%

Source: The 1986 *CAMPUS LIFE* survey of high school students. Includes multiple answers.

ior: "I wish people wouldn't use 'peer pressure' to excuse the drug or alcohol problem, because there is no such thing as peer pressure. How can someone make someone else do things against a person's will? But if a person gives in to this 'peer pressure,' then there must be some sort of inner insecurity or problem" (Female, 17, Ohio).

"Peer pressure is bull s——" (Female, 16, Michigan).

"Nobody I know ever pressures someone to drink if they don't want to" (Female, 16, Ohio).

"Peer pressure isn't always what it is made out to be. Many teens use this as an excuse. They want to try drugs or alcohol, and this is just a way of making themselves feel right about it. 'Well, my friends do it, so what would be wrong with me doing it' is sort of a cop-out" (Female, 17, Mississippi).

People (adults or teenagers) don't want to believe that someone else can make them do something. The idea of some invisible force out there twisting arms and pouring booze down unwilling throats seems ridiculous. However, peer pressure appears to be a bit more subtle than that. Take the fifteen-year-old girl from Ohio who caught the subtle inconsistency in her own friend's rationale for drinking: "I told someone who was getting drunk often that it wasn't cool and he laughed and said he didn't drink to be cool, but to have fun. But he then said he's only a *social drinker*." (Emphasis hers.)

Think about such phrases as "social drinker" and "everybody's doing it." Peer pressure doesn't mean guys jeering at the person who says, "No, thanks." What it does mean is an atmosphere in which drinking is acceptable, normal, even "cool." That, I think, is a truer, more realistic explanation of peer pressure. And it may also indicate why peer pressure's powerful influence is so hard to detect in our own lives.

Friendship Pressure

To give more insight into peer influence, students were asked, "If a friend asks you to go out drinking, do you say yes?" Seventy-one percent said they would go. This 71 percent is a combination of those who would: always go (8 percent), sometimes go (45 percent), and seldom go (18 percent).

The fact that over half say they will always or sometimes go out drinking when asked helps demonstrate the important part friends play in our decisions to drink. So it can be inferred that those students who shun peer pressure as their reason for drinking, insisting instead that they drink for fun, do so because their friends help define what things are fun. This seems to be supported by the fact that much teenage drinking takes place on weekends, often at parties. So a revised definition of peer pressure might be: It is "fun" (at least less uncomfortable) to do the "normal" thing.

It is interesting and important to note what happens when a student chooses not to go out drinking. About two out of five say there is no change in friendship when they refuse to go drinking. Only seven per-

GRAPH 11 **WILL GO DRINKING IF A FRIEND ASKS**

If someone you enjoy being with asks you to go out drinking with
him/her, do you say yes?

Always   50%   100%

■ 8%

Sometimes

■ 45%

Seldom

■ 18%

Never

■ 29%

Source: The 1986 *Campus Life* survey of high school students.

cent say they are "rejected" for saying they wouldn't go. So teenagers
should be encouraged. Rejection is not inevitable when they refuse to
drink with their friends.

That Macho Image

Closely associated with the issue of peer pressure is the feeling that
drinking proves manhood. One teenager put it pointedly and crudely
when he said that teens drink "to make them seem cool and not queer." If
students feel someone is less than a man or woman because he or she
doesn't drink, there is going to be a strong pull to, as one girl put it, "hold
a bottle of beer."

Why does drinking seem macho or cool? "TV commercials glorify
alcohol," said one seventeen-year-old girl from Iowa. "They make it
seem like you can't have a good time unless you're drinking. I know a lot
of teens deny that commercials have any effect on whether they drink or
not, but I think commercials really do [make a difference]."

The fairly recent popularity of wine coolers among youth most likely
can be attributed in part to some pretty slick ads. The power of advertising was vividly demonstrated by a group of thirty teenagers from Seattle
in a discussion they had about TV commercials. They were asked to
match a beer or cooler slogan with the beverage it represented. For instance, the match to "Give me a light" is: "Bud Light." The students
easily and quickly identified every slogan with its appropriate beverage.
After the "matching exercise," one of the guys said: "I think it's kind of
obvious how TV commercials have affected us, since we can all remember every single line and the specific beer you're talking about.
We've got to be aware of the things advertisers try to put into our heads."

During the course of this discussion, all but the two nondrinkers in the group admitted quite honestly to the effects of commercials on their drinking attitudes. Add peer pressure (as I have defined it) and curiosity to the persuasive nature of advertising, and there is obviously a powerful pull toward drinking.

Some Other Whys

A few students say that they personally drink alcohol "for taste," "to escape," "to feel good," "to relax," and "for special occasions." A very small number told me that they drink to "rebel," "to experiment," "to get drunk," or "out of curiosity." One reason for drinking that came up quite frequently along with other answers was boredom or "there's nothing to do." "People tell us to say 'no' but never give us fun alternatives," said one sixteen-year-old girl from Missouri. "What are we supposed to do? Food places, malls, parking lots don't always want us around."

RESPONSIBLE DRINKING?

Do teenagers believe there is such a thing as a responsible use of alcohol? Again, the feelings and opinions shifted radically when I moved from a discussion of drugs to drink.

GRAPH 12 **RESPONSIBLE DRINKING: YES OR NO?**

Is there such a thing as responsible use of alcohol?

YES	50%	100%
		75%
NO		
25%		

Source: The 1986 *Campus Life* survey of high school students.

While only a small group say there is such a thing as a responsible use of street drugs, around three-fourths of those surveyed believe there is a way to drink responsibly. And it should be pointed out that this number is quite a bit larger than the 44 percent who themselves drink. This could infer that some students who do not drink still feel other students can do so responsibly. Another factor could have been that the wording of the question did not differentiate between responsible drinking for adults and responsible drinking for teenagers. Students may have answered yes, thinking in terms of adult responsible drinking.

Students who say yes to responsible drinking give several conditions including:

GRAPH 13 **CONDITIONS FOR RESPONSIBLE DRINKING**

What are the conditions for "responsible drinking"?

Don't Overdo It   50%   100%

█████████████████████████████████ 75%

Don't Drink and Drive

████ 15%

Don't Hurt Anyone

██ 6%

Drink in the Presence of Adults

█ 3%

Don't Become an Alcoholic

▌ 1%

OTHER

█████ 16%

Source: The 1986 *CAMPUS LIFE* survey of high school students. Includes multiple answers.

Students' specific answers to the questions of responsible drinking include:

"As long as you're not endangering other people, you can have a drink now and then" (Male, 14, California).

"When responsible people drink, they aren't trying to get drunk, they are enjoying the taste" (Female, 14, Iowa).

"You should know how much you can handle" (Female, 16, Washington).

"When you drink beer and hard liquor to get drunk, you're a dork. If you drink alcohol for the taste (such as coolers and champagne) in reasonable amounts, it's OK. If you don't drive after drinking, you're cool" (Male, 18, Iowa).

"Don't let it get out of hand" (Male, 14, California).

"Know your limits and know when to stop" (Male, 18, California).

"If only a small amount is used for special occasions, that's responsible" (Female, 17, Iowa).

"Social drinking is OK, but drinking excessively is irresponsible" (Male, 15, California).

"Everything can be used for good as long as it's not used too much" (Female, 16, Washington).

"If you stay home and make everyone else with you spend the night, it's responsible. Do this so no one will drink and drive" (Female, 15, Iowa).

"Don't drink to get drunk" (Male, 16, Arizona).

"You should be able to use alcohol without doing it the wrong way" (Female, 16, Iowa).

"Limit yourself *before* you start drinking. If you're carpooling, have a designated driver who won't drink, so you can get home safely" (Female, 14, Iowa).

"It's OK to drink, just don't exceed the limits" (Male, 17, California).

"Drink in the privacy of your own home, not bothering anyone" (Female, 15, Arizona).

"Just don't get caught" (Male, 16, Iowa).

"Only have one drink" (Female, 18, Georgia).

"It is important to control your alcohol use" (Female, 14, Washington).

"I think it's OK to use alcohol to calm yourself down" (Male, 16, California).

"Use alcohol in small quantities and don't attempt to drive after drinking" (Male, 16, Arizona).

"I think there is such a thing as responsible drinking. I know people who drink sometimes but they're not alcoholics" (Male, 15, Washington).

"You must control the amount you drink" (Male, 16, Wisconsin).

"There is such a thing as a responsible use of alcohol: Drink socially and without getting out of hand" (Female, 14, Washington).

"Don't get drunk. Use alcohol in moderation" (Female, 16, Georgia).

"Small amounts" (Male, 17, Iowa).

"Yes, social drinking such as wine and champagne is a way to drink responsibly. People need to be aware of how much they are drinking and must limit themselves" (Female, 16, California).

"You'll be responsible if you drink enough just to get rowdy and in a great mood" (Female, 15, Wisconsin).

"Don't abuse it" (Male, 16, Wisconsin).

"Just don't get wasted" (Female, 15, Wisconsin).

"A person should know his or her limits on the consumption of alcohol, then only drink under those limits without getting drunk" (Male, 17, Iowa).

"If students go out to a party and just drink a little, not to get trashed, they can be responsible. They should also arrange for the driver to not drink" (Female, 17, Iowa).

"You should be careful not to overdo it, drive, or do anything that could harm another person" (Female, 16, California).

"Use alcohol, have a good time, don't get drunk, and don't drive after you use it" (Male, 17, Wisconsin).

"If you can have a drink because you want to and not just because everybody else is, I think that's being responsible" (Male, 17, Wisconsin).

"Very light social drinking or people who only drink on special occasions—that's responsible drinking" (Male, 17, Iowa).

"If people can drink it without getting high or being dependent on it, such as during meals" (Male, 16, California).

"I feel that sometimes adults believe that as soon as they see teenagers touch alcohol they are automatically alcoholics. This is totally untrue. My friends and I drink very rarely and are capable of controlling what we consume. We are not alcoholics, but we do drink. We don't drink to get drunk, either" (Female, 17, Chicago).

"Don't Overdo It"

More than three out of four students say that drinking in moderation ("Don't overdo it") is the best way to drink responsibly. Unfortunately, only a small number (15 percent) mentioned refusing to drink and drive as a way to show responsibility in drinking.

Other students added more stipulations to the idea of responsible drinking. "I would say that a communion service at a church or a glass of wine at dinner would be a responsible use," said a fifteen-year-old guy from Wisconsin. Others believe that adult use in moderation is acceptable, and oppose teenage drinking. A sixteen-year-old girl from Ohio commented, "I choose not to drink because I feel it is an adult custom."

The Casual Drinker

What is a casual or moderate drinker? Ask ten different people and you would probably get ten different answers. Some possible definitions include someone who:

- drinks once a month,
- drinks just on the weekends,
- drinks one drink a night,
- drinks only socially,
- never gets drunk,
- gets drunk only on special occasions,
- drinks moderately on holidays,

- drinks to excess only on holidays,
- drinks only when he or she wants to.

Of course, the list could go on and cover other ambiguous and unmeasurable areas. The point is, of course, that no one has very clearly defined what moderate use is.

If you drink, whether you are an adult or a teenager, I would challenge you to examine your reasons for drinking. To help you do this, answer the following questions. If you answer any of them with a "Yes," you may have good reasons to doubt that your drinking is completely "casual."

Do I often get drunk from alcohol?
Do I drink whenever friends want me to?
Have I ever driven after drinking?
Do I drink to escape problems?
Do I drink to catch a buzz?
Do I drink because my friends do?
Do I have to drink whenever I'm near alcohol?
Do I ever have a craving for a drink?
Is alcohol more to me than just a beverage?
Do I get some kind of a kick out of just having others see me with a cooler bottle or a beer can?
Is drinking an important part of my social life?

There are certainly other issues to consider. If you are a minor, there is always the problem of the legality of alcohol consumption. Then there is the question of your influence on others. If you have younger brothers and sisters or cousins, couldn't your drinking influence them to drink?

With this in mind, I have one more question for you to ask yourself: "Is my use—even my "casual use"—of alcohol helping or hindering the alcohol problem in my school, home, and community?"

TO YOUR HEALTH?

Some teenagers not only believe drinking alcohol is OK but they go a step further saying that alcohol use by teenagers can be a positive, healthy experience. Some even talk about alcohol being a good way to "flush out the kidneys." (Interestingly enough, alcohol abuse experts say this "flushing out" argument is simply a myth.) Other teens point to controversial studies linking moderate drinking to reduced heart disease, although those results are far from conclusive and not widely accepted by the medical community. Whatever their reasoning, the idea of "healthy moderate drinking" appears to be countered, at least for women, by a study released mid-1987 that links moderate drinking to breast cancer.

It's interesting that many drinkers don't believe alcohol quite fits in the dangerous substance category. One eighteen-year-old from Texas said, "Drinking is not harmful if it is controlled. Drugs cannot be controlled, so they are harmful all the time."

But many others do feel that alcohol represents a health hazard:

"Drinking doesn't seem like a very good way to take care of your body" (Female, 15, Idaho).

"I find that alcohol in no way benefits the user. It destroys him physically, emotionally, and spiritually" (Female, 17, Iowa).

"I don't drink because it's no good for the liver and I don't like the taste" (Female, 17, Georgia).

"While I do drink, I get worried because alcoholism runs in my family" (Female, 15, Missouri).

"I don't drink because, like drugs, alcohol is bad for you and I want to stay healthy. I might someday drink wine or champagne, but I don't plan on ever drinking regularly" (Female, 16, South Carolina).

"I don't drink because I want to be a healthy person" (Male, 17, Tennessee).

"I think it was really dumb to ban cigarette commercials from TV and still allow alcohol commercials when alcohol causes more deaths than cigarettes" (Female, 16, Texas).

"Drinking kills brain cells" (Female, 15, West Virginia).

"Drugs and alcohol should be abolished entirely. I've seen too many people hurt emotionally and physically by drugs and alcohol" (Female, 16, Washington).

"I've heard what alcohol can do to a teenager while he is growing up. I never could understand why anyone would want to drink that disgusting stuff" (Male, 15, South Carolina).

"Drinking is bad for your health; I have no use for it" (Female, 16, Georgia).

"Drinking is bad for your health and it is the cause of most teenage driving deaths" (Male, 14, Georgia).

"I'm diabetic and drinking would kill me. But even if it wouldn't kill me, I wouldn't drink" (Male, 17, Idaho).

"I don't drink because I'm an athlete and it's bad for my body" (Male, 16, South Carolina).

"I don't drink because I care about myself, and drinking isn't good for me in any way" (Female, 17, Georgia).

"Drinking messes up your stomach, it takes control over your mind, it eats your brain cells. It's bad for your health" (Female, 14, West Virginia).

"Drinking can eventually kill you emotionally and physically" (Female, 14, Georgia).

"I don't drink because I don't want to harm my body" (Female, 18, Idaho).

"My liver is good and I'd like it to stay that way" (Male, 17, Illinois).

"I'm afraid if I do drink I'll become addicted to it" (Female, 17, Georgia).

"Alcohol is not good for the body" (Male, 17, Illinois).

A Liquid Drug
To experts in the area of teenage alcohol abuse, arguments for moderate teenage alcohol use are purely academic. The National Council on Alcoholism points out that between four and five million youth currently suffer the negative consequences of alcohol abuse (this includes alcoholism, alcohol-related traffic accidents, recurring drunkenness, and poor grades resulting from abuse). One eighteen-year-old recovering alcoholic told me about the addictive power of alcohol in her own life:

> *I've never been able to understand people who think they can be social drinkers, who can go out to dinner and have one glass of wine just to drink. My attitude is, "Why don't you just drink pop, then?" When I drink it's to get drunk, period. If I drink just one drink I end up thinking I may as well get totally smashed. I had one relapse like that when I was in treatment. I was home on a pass for a weekend. I arrived at the airport and the drinking age there was eighteen. I spent thirty dollars on beer. I got so drunk. I kept calling my mom and telling her that my plane was delayed, and I ended up sitting at O'Hare Airport for three hours trying to sober up. It was real bad. I have never been able to sit down and have just one drink.*

According to experts in the field of alcohol abuse, even moderate drinking is harmful for teenagers. "There is no responsible use for alcohol among adolescents," one alcohol treatment specialist told me. "Alcohol is a depressant that affects the central nervous system just like the street drug Quaaludes." She went on to say that developing adolescent bodies are easily damaged through alcohol use. This specialist pointed out that alcoholic beverages—including beer and coolers—are danger-ous drugs. The only thing that makes alcohol legal for adults are "cultur-al and social traditions."

Many students, speaking merely from a medical standpoint, echo her concern and believe that alcohol is a drug to be avoided. One student even expressed concern over the fact that drugs and alcohol were placed in separate categories in the *Campus Life* survey: "Your questionnaire really angers me. Your attitude reminds me of the attitude held in my town. This attitude says alcohol is not a drug. Let me tell you, alcohol is a drug, not unlike marijuana or cocaine or LSD or crack."

Others expressed similar feelings:

"Alcohol is a liquid drug and it is as dangerous as any other drug" (Fe-male, 15, Washington).

"Alcohol is another form of drugs" (Female, 14, Missouri).

"Alcoholism is a disease, like drug addiction. So why not either legal-ize drugs or make alcohol illegal?" (Male, 16, Wisconsin).

"Alcohol is a drug. I don't care if you're smoking crack, smoking pot, or drinking, you get the same results no matter what. You get smashed either way. There's not much difference between an alcoholic and a drug addict" (Male, 16, Tennessee).

"Drinking is wrong; alcohol is a drug" (Female, 16, Georgia).

ADULT USE:
ANOTHER CASE OF "DO WHAT WE SAY, BUT. . ."?

For many teenagers, the inconsistency of adults in the area of alcohol use (and often drug use) is baffling. Though many teens accept that there's a difference between adult and teenage alcohol consumption, others feel this argument is just an excuse for adult irresponsibility:

"In filling out this survey it really makes me wonder: Why do I con-sume alcohol? It's really silly in a way. But then, why do adults drink?" (Female, 15, South Carolina).

"Adults drink to get buzzed. Why can't we?" (Male, 16, Michigan).

"I think most adults are hypocrites, because they say how bad it is to drink, but then they go out and get drunk. And I'm sure they partied in high school too" (Female, 14, Illinois).

"Teenagers see their parents and other adults drink, and they think, *Well, if Mom and Dad can do it, so can I.* Teenagers think it makes them more mature to go around town with a beer can in hand" (Female, 16, Texas).

"I've already been accepted to the college of my choice and I do fine in school. Why do adults try to tell us we have a problem? I smoke pot once a week and drink about the same. I have done lines [of cocaine] at homecoming and prom night, but I never drive under the influence. If you ask me, it's you [adults] who have the problem. You drink all the time and, unless you're so drunk that you can't stand up, you think you can drive. So get off my a—— and worry about yourself!" (Male, 18, Iowa).

"I, as a teenager, feel we are pressured into these things by our elders. Our elders want us to respect them, but how can we if they are drinking also?" (Female, 16, Ohio).

"Drug and alcohol problems start with adults. As long as teachers, doctors, administrators, and parents do them, kids will too" (Female, 16, Texas).

"A lot of adults supply minors [with alcohol]" (Female, 15, Minnesota).

"I think teens feel angry when it seems our generation is always being lectured. If we knew adults were having the same problems with drinking that we have, we wouldn't feel like we are always being picked on" (Female, 14, Washington).

"Until adults start being a better example for young people, they should stop being so hard on us and be more hard on themselves" (Male, 17, Texas).

"I believe adults should set examples for young people. When an adult preaches about alcohol or drugs while fixing himself a third martini, he's sending a message to his kid. Adults all say we're too young. Obviously this isn't the problem because the number of adult drug and alcohol users is just as staggering as the youth rate" (Female, 15, Ohio).

"Why focus on teenagers? Where do you think we learn all of this stuff? From adults" (Female, 17, Wisconsin).

"Our moms and dads drink, and most teenagers want to grow up to be like their parents" (Female, 16, Ohio).

Should Drinking Be Legal for All?

"Kids think that alcohol must be special," a sixteen-year-old guy from South Carolina remarked. "After all, look at the aura that adults have built around it. Kids know they can vote, be drafted, and be considered adults—but they cannot have a beer. This aura that adults have created around alcohol is what causes many of the problems."

How should this inconsistency between adult and teenage drinking ages be handled? By making consumption legal for minors? Nearly two teenagers in three would say no to such a proposal. According to a 1985 Gallup poll, 64 percent of the nation's teenagers support the enforcement of a twenty-one-year-old minimum drinking age. (Thirty-five percent believe the drinking age limit should be younger or nonexistent.)

CHART 2 MINIMUM AGE DRINKING LAW?

Should there be a 21-year-old minimum age drinking law?

	National Average	Male	Female	Ages 13-15	Ages 16-18
Favor	64%	61%	67%	68%	60%
Oppose	35%	39%	32%	31%	40%
No Opinion	1%	0%	1%	1%	0%

Source: *THE GALLUP YOUTH SURVEY* (1985). Used by permission from the Associated Press.

The *Campus Life* survey probed the age limit question a bit differently than the Gallup poll. It asked: "Should it be against the law for someone under eighteen to drink alcohol?" A total of 53 percent said yes to that question, with 40 percent believing that teens under eighteen should be able to drink legally.

GRAPH 14 SHOULD PEOPLE UNDER 18 DRINK?

Should it be against the law for somone under 18 to drink alcohol?

YES	50%	100%

53%

NO

40%

Other/No Opinion

7%

Source: The 1986 *CAMPUS LIFE* survey of high school students.

The 40 percent who would allow teenagers under eighteen to drink gave these types of reasons:

"People should be able to do it—it's their lives they'll ruin. Besides, legal or not, they'll drink anyway" (Female, 15, Ohio).

"Teenagers are rebellious and they enjoy going against authority. If drinking were legal it wouldn't be such a temptation. But we would drink anyway, even if it wasn't forbidden" (Female, 15, Ohio).

"It should be your choice whether or not to drink. But if you get caught drinking and driving, you're done" (Male, 15, Michigan).

"Teenagers will still drink whether or not it's against the law" (Female, 15, California).

"If you are old enough to open it, you can drink it" (Female, 14, Ohio).

"If people under eighteen want to drink, it's their decision. There shouldn't be anyone laying rules down" (Female, 17, Minnesota).

"I believe that if it were legal, people wouldn't do it as often. It wouldn't be a temptation" (Male, 15, Michigan).

"I don't think it should be illegal as long as you're not drinking and driving, and as long as you're under the supervision of parents" (Female, 17, Washington).

"I think it should be the person's choice whether or not to drink" (Female, 16, Wisconsin).

"Although alcohol is a drug, it is used more widely and better understood than street drugs. If they took the drinking age off, there wouldn't be such an emphasis on drinking and everyone would be equal" (Female, 16, Minnesota).

"I don't see anything wrong with drinking as long as teenagers can control themselves" (Female, 15, Texas).

"Even if you are underage, you can still get alcohol. It's all over. So why keep it illegal?" (Female, 17, South Dakota).

"It should be OK to drink with your parents during dinner" (Male, 16, Michigan).

"It should be legal, because some kids can handle it" (Female, 14, Washington).

Support Drinking for People Eighteen and Over
Many students expressed support for at least lowering the drinking age to eighteen in this way:

"If you are old enough to get killed serving in one of the Armed Forces, then you are old enough to drink" (Male, 15, Ohio).

"Eighteen-year-olds should be allowed to drink, because if they are old enough to fight in wars, to vote, and to be put in jail with older, more violent adults, the government should allow them to drink" (Male, 17, Texas).

"Eighteen is considered the age of a legal adult. You can serve your country and you are considered independent. You should be allowed to drink at that age" (Female, 17, Ohio).

"I think the drinking age is too high. I believe that if you have a say in what's going on in the United States through voting, you should be able to drink. By the time you're twenty, you can have a baby, own a house and a car, but you can't have a beer. Stupid, huh?" (Female, 18, Texas).

No to Legalized Drinking

However, more than half of those teenagers surveyed oppose legalized drinking for minors:

"It should be against the law for minors to drink. They do not know how to handle it" (Female, 17, Texas).

"People under eighteen are not mature enough to take responsibility for their use of alcohol" (Female, 17, Washington).

"It is hard for a teenager to realize that alcohol is addictive and habit-forming. It should be illegal for that reason" (Female, 17, Michigan).

"I think people under eighteen are too young to handle alcohol" (Female, 15, Texas).

"People under eighteen are still kids and they don't know how to handle being drunk. There are just too many accidents involving teenagers who have been drinking" (Female, 14, Washington).

"There are too many teenage accidents because of alcohol—too much violence" (Male, 17, Texas).

"People under eighteen are not mature enough to handle drinking" (Male, 16, Michigan).

"Drinking should be illegal for people under eighteen because it can harm you" (Female, 15, Ohio).

"People under eighteen are still wild kids and anything seems easy for them to do when drinking" (Female, 17, Washington).

"Teenagers cannot handle liquor as well as adults" (Male, 18, Texas).

"If you are under eighteen, you can't control yourself as well as adults can" (Female, 16, Wisconsin).

"I think those under eighteen often get alcohol and can't control themselves while drinking. If stricter laws were enforced, then the problem wouldn't be as tragic" (Female, 16, Missouri).

"If they have to wait maybe they'll have plenty of time to think twice before drinking at a later age" (Female, 17, Washington).

"Young people are not able to handle such a big responsibility as being allowed to drink. They do not know when to stop" (Female, 18, Texas).

"A lot of people aren't mature. They don't realize the harm they can cause another person or themselves" (Female, 15, Washington).

"Teenagers under eighteen are not capable of understanding when to quit and what happens when you drink. Whereas adults can judge better" (Female, 17, Ohio).

"Your body is not physically mature enough to handle alcohol and there is a tendency to drink more to impress people" (Male, 17, Washington).

"If it weren't illegal, kids would be coming to school drunk" (Male, 15, Washington).

Uptight in America?

Another inconsistency teenagers point to is the difference between the drinking laws in the U.S. and in other countries. Specifically, they want to know why teenage consumption is allowed over there, but not here. Some of the arguments these students give include:

"I have friends from New Zealand and Mexico and it's not uncommon for kids to have a drink with coaches, parents, and friends. If you don't restrict things from kids, the newness and excitement wears off in a while" (Male, 17, Washington).

"In Europe the age for drinking is legal at a much younger age. In Europe they don't have the drinking problem we do" (Female, 17, South Dakota).

"I personally feel that no drinking age is necessary—there isn't one in Europe and they have no alcohol problem" (Female, 17, Iowa).

"What matters is how alcohol is viewed. Europe is an excellent example. But in this country we have made it taboo, so people want to experiment" (Male, 17, South Dakota).

"Look at France. They don't have a drinking age and they don't have half the problem with it as the U.S." (Female, 16, Ohio).

"In many countries, Mexico for example, there is no drinking age. If teens want alcohol, they can get it. Why be sneaky about it?" (Female, 16, Wisconsin).

"In other countries kids are allowed to drink, but in this country if you do it's a crime. By having restrictions it makes drinking more fun to do" (Male, 17, Washington).

It's true that these are some interesting points. But they bring up an even more interesting question: Are other countries problem free? In a word, no. While problems may not show up in the same way as they do in the U.S., other countries have their own share of troubles related to alcohol abuse. One seventeen-year-old girl from South Dakota points to the social acceptability of drinking in Europe, then adds, "But life expectancy is much shorter in Europe and there are many more alcoholics." She has a good point.

In terms of alcohol consumption alone, consider this 1976 study done for the *Encyclopedia of Alcoholism:* Out of twenty-six countries, France ranked highest in per capita consumption of alcohol, Portugal second, Spain third, and Luxembourg fourth. The United States ranked twenty-second in per capita consumption. And in terms of deaths through the alcohol-related disease, cirrhosis of the liver, a study released in 1974 says that among men, Chile ranked first in per capita deaths, Portugal second, and France third. The United States ranked tenth.

Alcohol-related highway accidents offer further insight. According to a 1979 study done by the Canada-based Addiction Research Council, the number of alcohol-related traffic accidents in Austria was 56.1 per 100,000 people. In West Germany it was 23.5 per 100,000, and in the United States it was 9.2 per 100,000.

A 1979 survey of West Germans showed increasing public awareness of the alcohol abuse problem in that country. In a poll of 2,000 Germans, 56 percent said they were concerned about the high consumption of alcohol. According to the *Encyclopedia of Alcoholism,* "This figure represents a significant increase over the 31 percent who expressed concern in an inquiry made five years earlier." Sixty-seven percent of the respondents to this study also said they recommended a strict ban on allowing children to have alcohol, while only 52 percent had recommended such a prohibition five years before. Since awareness of alcoholism and alcohol-related diseases is increasing in Germany, I would expect those percentages to be even higher today.

IS EXPERIENCE THE BEST TEACHER?
Another question from the survey is: "If a teenager has seen first-hand a tragedy caused by drug or alcohol use, will it curb personal use?" Here are some of the comments from teens who said yes:

"I don't drink because I have seen what damage it can do to people" (Male, 17, Georgia).

"I have never used drugs or alcohol because I have seen what they do to you" (Female, 14, Georgia).

"My uncle got messed up real bad once, and addiction usually runs in the family. I don't want to follow the rest of the family" (Male, 15, West Virginia).

"I don't use drugs or alcohol. Too many people close to me have been hurt because of drugs. I have seen too many people killed because of alcohol" (Female, 15, Tennessee).

"I don't drink because my dad was killed by a drunken driver and I don't want to have anything to do with the stuff that killed him" (Male, 17, Georgia).

"I despise alcohol because a close friend was killed by a drunken driver" (Female, 15, Michigan).

"I've seen and heard about many things that drinking can do to you and your body, and it's pretty gross" (Female, 14, Washington).

"When I see my friend high, it makes me feel stronger against use. I wish she would get some help" (Female, 14, Washington).

"The main reason I say no to alcohol is because one of my best friends and I came very close to being killed the night after the Fourth of July this past summer. Some drunk, a twenty-three-year-old woman, was going about fifty M.P.H. and rear-ended me while I was at a stop light. The only reason I am here to tell about it is because of the seat belt I was wearing. Also, many of my friends have been killed or seriously hurt through drunken driving accidents. Drinking just is not worth a person's well-being—or life, for that matter" (Female, 18, Montana).

"I don't care for drinking because it isn't worth it. I have had two members of my family killed because of drug- and alcohol-related accidents. I can't take the risk. I couldn't imagine what my parents would do if I died because of alcohol or drugs" (Male, 16, Nevada).

"Someone very close to me drinks alcohol and I don't want what's happening to him to happen to me" (Female, 15, Illinois).

"I am against drugs and alcohol because my cousin went out celebrating after a dance and he drank too much beer. Afterward he went driving around with his friends and got into a car accident. He was rushed to the hospital, but he was injured so bad that he died after he was in the hospital two hours" (Female, 14, Texas).

"In my freshman year of high school, a friend of mine had a bad acid trip. He never came back. Since that time, I've said no to drugs" (Female, 16, Texas).

"I say no and do not ever drink because my dad is an alcoholic and I feel strongly that I do not want to end up as he did" (Female, 17, Texas).

Awareness Not Enough?
Unfortunately, while I have no hard statistics on how well experience teaches against abuse, the attitudes of many youth seem to be reflected in what one sixteen-year-old guy from Missouri said: "Teens are so much

more aware these days of the dangers, but don't seem to take them seriously." Regarding drinking and driving, the *Campus Life* survey indicates that many more youth consider "not overdoing it" a more important consideration than driving under the influence. Looking a bit more optimistic, a 1985 youth Gallup poll shows some decline between 1984 and 1985 in the number of teenagers who rode with a driver who had been drinking, and in the number of teenagers who drove a car shortly after drinking. So increased awareness may be having a slight impact.

CHART 3 **DRINKING AND DRIVING**

	National Average	Male	Female	Ages 13–15	Ages 16–18
Passenger in car driven by person own age who had been drinking					
1984	36%	35%	36%	17%	54%
1985	28%	28%	27%	15%	40%
Drove car shortly after drinking					
1984	14%	19%	9%	2%	24%
1985	8%	9%	8%	1%	15%

Source: *THE GALLUP YOUTH SURVEY* (1985). Used by permission from the Associated Press.

Why Don't We Learn?
Some teenagers feel frustrated that friends, or that they themselves, don't "live and learn." This is summed up well by a seventeen-year-old girl from Washington:

> *This past year when I was a sophomore was very difficult for my friends and me. We lost one of our very close friends due to drinking and driving. He was not driving, but he was intoxicated and with a bunch of other friends. When I first learned of his death, I could not accept it. I always thought it happened to kids who were jerks and had nothing going for themselves. But my special friend had every-*

thing going for him. He was on the diving team, active in choir, good looks, fantastic personality, popularity. I could go on and on forever.

Now that he is dead you would think we would have learned from other people's mistakes. But the kids in my school have not. Sure, at the time of my special friend's death everyone said, "I will never drink again as long as I live." That remark only lasted about two weeks after his funeral. It seemed like everyone went back to doing what they liked doing best: Drinking.

I felt so angry, so confused. How could people possibly start drinking when one of their closest friends just died from drinking? It was pretty sickening to watch what my friends were doing.

I stopped drinking for about six months after my friend's funeral. To be totally honest, I started to drink occasionally with my friends because in May, school was coming to an end. I thought I would party with my friends for one last time. In late May, a lot of my friends were going to graduate and on graduation night it was a nightmare relived all over again. One of my friends went out drinking that night and was riding with another girl who was driving while intoxicated. She drove into a ditch and killed my friend. Since then I have not and never will drink again. It is sad that two of my good friends had to die to stop me from drinking. How many friends do we have to lose before we'll stop?

THREE

REASONS NOT TO USE

VALUES, FAITH, DREAMS, AND MORE

In my interactions with teenagers, I discovered a small minority who have given considerable thought to why they don't use either drugs or alcohol. One fifteen-year-old girl from Michigan pinpoints fear of addiction as a chief concern: "Some of my friends do drugs and drink, and invited me to do the same. But I refused. They respected my decision and we are still good friends. If more people would refuse more often, there would be fewer druggies and alcoholics."

Yet, many in the 56 percent who claim not to drink give general reasons such as "have no desire," "don't like the taste," or "never been offered." Health concerns and fear of alcoholism rated quite low, giving a rather dismal picture of current alcohol education. And a great number of teens simply don't give a reason for why they don't drink or use drugs.

It is not always easy to tell those who say no from those who say no *and mean it,* especially when push comes to shoving a beer can in the hand. Take "fear of getting caught"—a rather tenuous reason for not using. Fear based on punishment is not an internalized value, a value chosen because of personal conviction and commitment. "I don't drink," a fourteen-year-old girl from Missouri said, "because if my parents found out I'd be dead meat." It's probable that when her source of fear is removed, she will have no real reason to abstain. For instance, if she

GRAPH 15 **REASONS FOR NOT DRINKING**

Why do you choose not to drink?

No Desire   50%   100%

42%

Unhealthy/Dangerous

5%

Don't Like the Taste

5%

Drinking Can Mess Up Your Life

5%

Fear Becoming an Alcoholic

6%

Moral/Religious Reasons

2%

Not Available/Not Offered

2%

Because of Sports

1%

Fear Losing Control

1%

Unspecified Fear

1%

It's Stupid

1%

Fear Getting Caught

1%

(The students who choose not to drink—56 percent of those surveyed—give these reasons. Not all answers are represented; many simply chose not to give an answer as to why they don't drink.)

Source: The 1986 *CAMPUS LIFE* survey of high school students.

leaves home to begin college a state or two away she probably will have less fear of punishment.

Teens who refer to taste, lack of desire, and inability to get alcohol, or who list no reason for avoiding drinking, could most likely be convinced to drink if it seemed right to do so in a certain situation. This lack of conviction probably accounts for the tendency of younger teenage nondrinkers to become drinkers later in high school.

In contrast, those who have well thought-out value systems and those who present creative alternatives to drug and alcohol use have the great-

GRAPH 16 **REASONS FOR NOT USING DRUGS**

Why have you never used drugs?

No Desire	50%	100%

70%

Unhealthy/Dangerous
20%

Drugs Are Stupid
12%

Fear of Addiction
10%

Drugs Mess Up Your Life
9%

Unspecified Fear
5%

Fear of Losing Control
4%

Moral/Religious Reasons
3%

Bad Side Effects
3%

Because of Sports
2%

Friends Don't Do It
2%

Not Available/Not Offered
1%

Fear of Getting Caught
1%

Too Expensive
1%

(Of those surveyed, 73 percent said they don't use drugs. Includes multiple answers.)

Source: The 1986 *CAMPUS LIFE* survey of high school students.

est chance of sticking with their decision to abstain. The following are some reasons and comments expressed by such teens—reasons that show some depth of conviction:

They want to be in control. Many students acknowledge that alcohol consumption and drug use means a loss of self-control. This inability to be in charge of one's own actions keeps many students from abuse.

"I like to feel in control of my life and drugs and alcohol don't give me that control" (Female, 15, South Carolina).

"Why don't I drink? I watch my friends make fools of themselves and I don't want to be like that" (Female, 17, South Carolina).

"Drinking makes you out of control. I want to always know what I am doing" (Female, 16, Georgia).

"I don't want to make an a—— out of myself, like I see people doing under the influence" (Female, 16, California).

"I like to know what I am doing all the time" (Male, 16, South Carolina).

They feel self-sufficient, personally secure. Time and again, former heavy users of both drugs and alcohol told me about their feelings of inadequacy and low self-worth. On the other hand, many nonusers feel good about themselves; they have no need to use drugs or alcohol to find acceptance or to "improve" their personalities.

"If drinking is what it takes to be accepted, I'd rather stay away and be rejected" (Male, 16, California).

"I don't need to drink or get high to have a good time. Anyway, what could drugs do for me that I can't do for myself?" (Female, 16, Michigan).

"I think that if any person needs to use alcohol or drugs, they are just afraid of life" (Female, 18, Texas).

"I have realized that you don't have to drink to be considered in the in-crowd" (Male, 16, California).

"I have never used alcohol, drugs, or cigarettes and I'm fine. I don't understand why other people use them. I guess I have learned to live through my problems and I believe others can too" (Female, 17, Washington).

"Sometimes you get the urge to do what your friends do, but I feel that being an individual is best" (Female, 17, California).

"Many say they drink to have a good time. But I feel they're just running away from themselves and trying to be someone and something they're not" (Female, 16, Washington).

"Drinking does not make me a more important person" (Male, 16, Georgia).

They feel responsible toward themselves and others. Nonusers often feel an inner drive to avoid the personal and societal troubles that come with substance abuse. They may feel their world, friendships, schools, communities, and families are better off because they do not drink or use drugs.

"Drinking can lead to worse things that will eventually harm me and others" (Female, 14, Georgia).

"Alcohol only causes problems, it doesn't solve them" (Male, 14, Idaho).

"I have too many obligations to get myself messed up in drugs and alcohol" (Female, 16, California).

"If I drank I could possibly take somebody's life out on the highway" (Male, 17, Georgia).

"Getting high is a lifetime choice, not a thrill for one night. Your decision to use drugs not only affects you now, it stays with you for the rest of your life" (Female, 16, Washington).

"I don't need alcohol for anything. I have more sense than to drink and risk the life of a stranger or myself" (Male, 16, Georgia).

They have positive family relationships and friendships. Loyalty to and respect for friends and family keep certain students from using drugs and alcohol.

"My parents, especially my mother, are really special to me. I know some people who think alcohol will cure all their problems with their parents, so they stab their parents right in the back. I could never do that. I know parents don't say things just for their health, but because they love us and want the best for us" (Female, 18, South Dakota).

"My mom and dad did not bring me up to think that drinking is OK" (Male, 15, Ohio).

"It's a matter of family pride and pride in one's own self" (Female, 15, South Carolina).

"My parents and my friends have influenced me greatly on my decision to say no. I have never had any trouble saying no because I know what's good and bad for me" (Female, 17, Texas).

They have goals, priorities, and dreams. A 1986 survey of students in the "high achievers" category indicates that 57 percent say they either have never had an alcoholic beverage or have tried alcohol but don't currently drink. Only 14 percent state that they drink more than once a month. These high achievers also say they don't use drugs. Ninety-three percent do not use marijuana. The percentage who do not use other drugs is even higher. The point: Academically oriented students generally have strong personal goals and often avoid substance abuse. While I can't be sure that the students below fall into the "high achievers" group, they certainly represent students with dreams for the future—dreams they won't let alcohol or drugs destroy.

"I don't drink because I have my whole life ahead of me" (Female, 14, Tennessee).

"I don't need drugs for anything. I want to be the best I can be" (Male, 14, Georgia).

"It ruins too many opportunities in life" (Male, 15, Georgia).

"I don't use drugs and alcohol because if I got hooked on them they could ruin my future" (Female, 15, South Carolina).

"I feel that teenagers should set goals for themselves; when they do this they find that drinking or drugs won't fit into those goals" (Female, 15, South Carolina).

"I don't want to waste my life. I think that I have better use for my time than messing up my life with drugs and alcohol" (Female, 14, Georgia).

Seeking alternatives. Many teen drug and alcohol users often cite boredom as a reason for drinking alcohol or using drugs; many nonusers emphasize their ability to have fun without substance abuse.

"I don't need to be drunk to have fun. I have just as much fun as any drunken person and I can remember the fun in the morning" (Female, 16, Georgia).

"I feel I can have fun without using drugs or alcohol" (Female, 16, Wisconsin).

"It would help students if they knew that fun doesn't mean doing things that are wrong" (Female, 17, Washington).

"The friends I have are those who I generally consider to be like me. We all take school seriously, yet we still have lots of fun away from books and school; we all have some sort of goal in our lives such as college, a good job, even the Air Force Academy; we all are involved in sports, jobs, church youth group, or clubs. We have varying interests and we have each other.

"Several of my friends come from troubled or splitting homes, yet none of them drink or do drugs. We all know the consequences and have chosen other options at rough points in our lives. We don't want to become dependent on something as harmful as drugs.

"I guess it would be good just not to have a lot of free time on your hands. Maybe boredom is what drives some kids into drugs" (Female, 17, Texas).

They have religious beliefs. Mention "the Christian perspective on alcohol consumption," and many people imagine the wild-eyed, hatchet-brandishing female teetotaler of the early 1900s. While the hatchets have been long buried, the American temperance movement has affected and continues to influence the stance many religious groups take on alcohol. For example, some Christian denominations and churches even oppose communion wine, opting for grape juice instead.

While some, like teetotaler John the Baptist, chose abstinence for religious reasons, others in Bible times drank wine. Even Jesus did not abstain, though it brought condemnation from some members of the religious community. "For John the Baptist came neither eating bread nor drinking wine, and you say, 'He has a demon,'" Jesus once said. "The Son of Man [referring to himself] came eating and drinking, and you say, 'Here is a glutton and a drunkard'" (Luke 7:33). On one occasion, Jesus even turned water into wine for a wedding celebration (John 2:1-11).

Like in Bible times, some Christians today choose total abstinence (with the possible exception of communion wine). These believers take their stance for social and ethical reasons. Some believe the current image of alcohol as presented by advertisers and the media in general is a long way from the image of wine that existed in Jesus' day. They believe such media misrepresentations encourage abuse and misuse. They take their stance against drinking because of the terrible tragedies it can create: alcoholism, highway deaths, child and spouse abuse, etc.

Other Christians are more relaxed about the issue and see social drinking as acceptable. Yet while Christians, along with followers of the Jewish faith, vary in their attitudes regarding alcohol use, there is consensus among these various traditions that drunkenness is not acceptable behavior. Here are some of the Bible passages (to which I have added italics for emphasis) used to support this claim:

> Do not join with those who *drink too much wine . . . for drunkards . . .* become poor, and drowsiness clothes them in rags. (Prov. 23:20-21)
> You must not associate with anyone who calls himself a brother but is sexually immoral or greedy, an idolater or a slanderer, *a drunkard* or a swindler. (1 Cor. 5:11)
> The acts of the sinful nature are obvious: sexual immorality, impurity and debauchery; idolatry and witchcraft; hatred, discord, jealousy, fits of rage, selfish ambition, dissensions, factions and envy; *drunkenness,* orgies, and the like. I warn you, as I did before, that those who live like this will not inherit the kingdom of God." (Gal. 5:19-21)

Do not get *drunk on wine,* which leads to debauchery [immorality].
(Eph. 5:18)
You are all sons of the light and sons of the day. We do not belong to
the night or to the darkness. So then, let us not be like others. . . . For
. . . *those who get drunk, get drunk at night.* But since we belong to
the day, let us be self-controlled. (1 Thess. 5:5-8)

I find it interesting that "drunkenness" is included with such sins as
witchcraft, hatred, sexual immorality, and idol worship. Today's religious community continues to oppose drunkenness, while extending
help and social services to individuals and families suffering from problems created by alcohol abuse.

This concern about abuse is held by at least some youth in the religious community. As I mentioned in the introduction, a special survey
appeared in *Campus Life* magazine that asked readers about their drinking habits. A largely Christian-oriented group, these readers showed
some differences from the general high school population. While
around 17 percent claim to drink occasionally, 55 percent say they have
never drunk, and another 24 percent say they seldom drink. Only 4 percent drink at least once a week.

Avoidance of drug use is also high among this group of Christian students, with more than 92 percent claiming never to have used illegal
drugs. This contrasts with the 72 percent in the general high school population who claim to have never used an illegal substance.

The *Campus Life* magazine survey found that 45 percent of religious-
oriented students claim to drink. Even if that drinking is done moderately (as is possibly the case for the 24 percent who "seldom drink"), those
students would still have trouble reconciling their use with the Christian
belief that keeping the law is important. Face it, minors who drink are
breaking the law. Several Christian students wrote me long letters about
the guilt they feel because of their drinking habits. Many evangelical
Christian students believe their faith does not condone drinking, yet feel
driven for various reasons (including peer pressure) to consume alcohol.

It is important to note that only 2 percent of the students in high school
surveys listed "religious reasons" as their reason for not drinking. This is
quite low considering Gallup research which says 22 percent of the nation's teenagers claim that "religious beliefs are the most important influence" in their lives (from a 1977 to 1983 study). Possibly, this 22
percent hold "untested" beliefs. If the Gallup survey had asked more
specific questions in the area of alcohol attitudes, it might have found a

CHART 4 **COMPARISON OF STUDENTS FROM A RELIGIOUS BACKGROUND TO THE GENERAL HIGH SCHOOL POPULATION**

RELIGIOUS BACKGROUND	55% Never Drink
	24% Seldom Drink
	4% Drink Once a Week
	17% Drink Occasionally
	92% Never Used Illegal Drugs
GENERAL HIGH SCHOOL POPULATION	56% Rarely or Never Drink
	27% Drink on Weekends
	73% Never Used Illegal Drugs

(Religious background represents students who responded to a survey placed in *Campus Life* magazine. The survey may be skewed in comparison to the general religious population due to methodology. Unlike the other *Campus Life* surveys, the magazine survey was not a cross section of the population—even of the religious population. It circulated among students from a largely "evangelical," conservative Christian background.)

Source: The 1986 *CAMPUS LIFE* survey of high school students and the 1986 *CAMPUS LIFE* magazine survey of students from a religious background.

smaller percentage of students who claim that faith influences their lives in that particular area. Further, what does "influence" mean? That it keeps them from doing something or that it makes them feel guilty after doing it?

Still, we shouldn't simply write off the 2 percent on the *Campus Life* surveys who oppose drinking for religious reasons. As small as it may be, it does represent a vocal and religiously committed group of students. Here are some of their comments:

"Using drugs and alcohol is stupid because it destroys your body, and I am a Christian, therefore I feel drug and alcohol use is wrong" (Male, 17, South Carolina).

"I stopped drinking because of my religion" (Female, 17, Nevada).

"I'm trying to live my life for the Lord, and I can't do that if I'm high on drugs or alcohol" (Female, 14, Georgia).

"Drinking and drugs are against church standards" (Male, 16, Idaho).

"I'm a born-again Christian who believes God fills the voids in our lives—not drugs or alcohol" (Female, 18, Iowa).

"Drinking is against my religion and it doesn't fit into my ethics" (Male, 16, Idaho).

"My faith plays a big part in my stand against drugs and alcohol. Believing that I don't need these things, that I have something higher and something above to base my life on, keeps me from needing alcohol as a crutch. Peer pressure doesn't get to me, I think, because of my belief. I don't think that makes me a big deal. But my faith plays a big part in my stand" (Female, 16, Tennessee).

"Using drugs and drinking alcohol are things that God would not be pleased with because drugs are not good for me, and my body is the temple of God" (Female, 15, Illinois).

"God doesn't approve" (Female, 16, Georgia).

"Drinking and using drugs are sins against God" (Male, 15, Colorado).

"I am a Christian and I can't understand why any person would want to drink or take drugs. The only things that can come out of it are death, a miserable life, poor relationships with family and friends. And if you're taking drugs or drinking alcohol, I don't see how you could have a meaningful or good relationship with God" (Female, 14, Washington).

"Drug and alcohol use is against my religion and my principles" (Female, 14, Missouri).

"The Bible says not to do things that would harm you" (Male, 16, Missouri).

"I feel sorry for people who turn to drugs instead of to God!" (Female, 15, California).

AN ARGUMENT AGAINST COMMON "EXCUSES"
One teenager, who was a part of the *Campus Life* magazine survey of religious students, wrote me an open letter. What follows is her perspective:

> *Everyone who drinks seems to have a good reason. But when you think about it, all the reasons are just excuses. There are good alternatives.*
>
> *Some say they drink to celebrate or have fun. However, there are other ways to celebrate that are more rewarding and a lot healthier than drinking. Whatever happened to ordering pizza and Cokes? They certainly taste better than alcohol. And besides, when was the last time you heard of someone getting addicted to or getting a hangover from Pepsi?*
>
> *Some drink to get rid of their problems. But does it really work?*

Sure, you may forget your problems for a night. But the next day, when your headache goes away and you stop throwing up, all the problems you had yesterday are still there.

If people say they drink to be happy, they have serious problems. The happy feeling doesn't last long. If you can't be happy and sober at the same time, then your problems run deeper than alcohol can solve.

Some say they drink to relax. Well, that's a partially [true] reason. Alcohol is a depressant and does cause relaxation. So much relaxation that it slurs speech and keeps you from driving in a straight line. If you can't relax in a group unless you drink, then you should find another group that you can feel more at ease with.

If people drink to be accepted, they are looking for the wrong kind of friends. They should try to find friends who will accept them as they are. They should not have to buy friendship by drinking.

It is a good idea to avoid drinking if you have to drive. And it is good for one or two people to stay sober at a party, so other people will have a safe ride home. Or is that just an excuse? Maybe teenage drinkers are just afraid to say, "No, thanks. I don't drink."

NO LONGER USING: PERSPECTIVES OF FORMER DRUG AND ALCOHOL ABUSERS

I spent many hours listening to the stories of former drug abusers and nondrinking alcoholics. Many students would write these people off as "burnouts" or "dirtballs," but during my time with these teens I discovered individuals who certainly don't deserve such insensitive put-downs. Yes, they have problems and deeply troubled pasts. But they also are individuals with deep feelings, goals, and an ever-growing understanding of themselves and their personal worth. And, beyond the highly emotional horror stories these teens can tell, they have profound insights into why it is important to avoid the use of alcohol and drugs. These insights deserve consideration by users and nonusers alike.

For this particular section I have chosen five people who met the following requirements: 1) Has undergone treatment for abuse of drugs, or alcohol, or both; 2) Continues to be involved in counseling or a support group such as AA (Alcoholics Anonymous) or NA (Narcotics Anonymous); 3) Was not using at the time of the interview. Here are their personal insights into how they became abusers, why they now choose to avoid abuse, and how they go about living drug and alcohol free lives.

Mark[1]: "Sick and Tired of Being Sick and Tired"

Mark, a sixteen-year-old junior, speaks with a soft southern drawl and has sky-blue eyes; he is a pleasant, likable guy with long, reddish-blond hair and a tall, lanky frame. When we met, he was wearing a black T-shirt, blue jeans, and a denim jacket. He currently serves as a group leader in a peer counseling program for drug and alcohol abusers. About his involvement in helping abusers, Mark told me, "If I can help one person in that group I'll be the happiest man alive. Just one person and I'll be satisfied."

For Mark, the abuse story started at a fairly early age:

When I was eleven or twelve, I started using drugs. I smoked a lot of marijuana and did a lot of speed. And then after a while that wasn't enough, so I got into alcohol and started doing street drugs and alcohol at the same time. I used the stuff all the time. At school, after school, weekends, always. Parties—I always found a party. I would say I stayed stoned 90 percent of the time for about five years.

During this time, one of my best friends got killed in a car wreck and another friend was in a coma for about four months because of drug abuse, and that kind of hit home. But I still wouldn't quit. Then I got kicked out of school. I was always getting in trouble with the law. And since my dad and I were using together, it caused continual tension at home with my mom. One day all hell broke loose at home. I just got tired of the whole mess. There is this thing in AA that goes, "Sick and tired of being sick and tired," and that was it. I was just tired of it. It got to where instead of having fun and getting high to get rid of the pain, I was just causing more pain by getting high. When that starts happening you'd better stop or you're going to die [from the drugs] or commit suicide—one of the two.

I went into a treatment center a few months back. I've been straight ever since. I haven't failed any yet. I don't know how I haven't. I've made it by the skin of my teeth. What really helps a lot is going to AA and NA meetings. It helps to get involved with a group of people who are trying to do the same things you are. It makes it easier.

It also helps to get away from old friends. You have to. There is no way possible a person can stay straight and hang around with the same people they did when they used drugs or drank. Fellow users and drinkers aren't true friends anyway.

[1]Real names have not been used

I must also stay away from certain places. I used to go to the vocational school and I can't go there anymore. I used to get high there every day and it brings back too many old memories.

For anyone who is using or drinking at all I would say, "Stop before you get yourself in trouble." That's the way I started, just using every now and then. You have to set your priorities straight. You have to know you can't get high and you have to know what's going to happen if you do. For an alcoholic and a drug addict—after they stop—going back and doing drugs or drinking alcohol is worse than death.

Wisdom comes with experience. I'm glad that I've had this experience because now I am a better person for it. I know what it's like being down there. Now I can try to help people so they don't make the same mistakes, 'cause it was a living hell being down so far that you don't care about anything anymore—not yourself or anything.

Cassey: "Look for Straight Friends"

Cassey, eighteen years old and a recent high school graduate, is full of life and energy. When we got together to talk, she moved quickly into the room without a hint of past insecurities, introduced herself, and put me immediately at ease. Currently she is working with deaf kids who have drug problems. She also attends a small city college. "Someday," Cassey explained, "I hope to be working either in a treatment center or as a probation officer. Most of all, I want to be successful in terms of living a good life, being off drugs—not problem free, because no one is free of their problems. But I've learned that problems are a blessing. They've helped me grow, and I learn from my mistakes and learn to deal with my problems better. I just want to be successful and happy with me."

Finding that happiness will require a lot of work, considering what Cassey has to say about her past:

It's the norm in my family to drink to solve your problems. You see, everybody in my family except my mother has been touched with the disease of alcoholism. Along with that, my mother and I haven't ever been able to communicate and we fight all the time. Never have I felt like I could come to her and say, "I'm scared," or "I'm having a problem." I have always had a hard time expressing my feelings to my family or to anyone else.

In school I always lived in fear of being alone. I also had a lot of hate and mistrust toward authority figures. So when it came time to find a group to belong to I knew the burnouts were my most logical choice. There I found instant popularity. By the time I was thirteen, I was totally hooked on drugs. I thought I couldn't have fun without them. I thought that people who didn't do drugs were weird. I just wanted to live in the fast lane and be crazy.

As my habit increased my problems grew. I got kicked out of high school a couple of times, so I began running away from home and getting into LSD, heroin, and cocaine. I was also selling drugs and stealing a lot. I even stole my mother's car once. I was always in trouble. I always had the feeling that everybody was against me.

My mother ended up having me put into a detox center to get some help. I didn't get a lot out of the first one I was at because I didn't want to give up anything. To me drugs were a protection, a shield against the pain I felt inside. I also didn't want to give up my old friends. Eventually, I was placed in another treatment center in Texas far away from old friends for about a year and a half. The counselors there helped me learn to talk about my feelings and open up and be honest with people. That wasn't easy, because I was so used to hiding from everything. At one point, it became unbearable. I just couldn't deal with all these negative feelings I had about my family. I just wanted to die, so I tried to kill myself again and again through overdosing on drugs I could get smuggled in. Finally, though, the pain and hurt became less intense and I began to handle my problems through talking them out. In time I discovered I didn't need drugs anymore.

What people really need to understand is that the best way to avoid use is just stay away from drugs and alcohol. As a former abuser, I know this is essential. I also know it's not easy to keep away from the stuff. When I get upset I want to get drunk or something. I don't think about doing drugs anymore, though. Sometimes I wish I could be a social drinker, but I really know that's not possible.

It's also critical to look for straight friends. Drug friends are not really friends. They just use each other for drugs or money. One day I overdosed on LSD and I can remember being very scared and crying to this friend of mine and she said, "Don't cry, you're a baby." I finally realized that this girl wasn't a real friend. If I would have had someone I could really talk to, someone who said, "You don't have to be any special way to be my friend," I don't think I would have gotten into drugs.

AA serves as my group of friends now. We meet regularly to talk *about staying off drugs and alcohol, and how to help each other find better ways of coping. It's a group I can go to and say, "I'm struggling," and the other people can say, "So am I," or "I was there, let me help you." It's all confidential and it's real nice. We are all on a first-name basis. I know without it, I would really be struggling, because I don't think you can go to a detox center and come out and be OK for life. It takes a long time and a support group of some kind. I'm still struggling and I've been in these AA meetings for almost three years now.*

John: "It Was Time for an Image Change"

When we were together, John's brown eyes were watery and seemed to look through me, as though he was concentrating on the postered wall of the high school counseling office. His green Ralph Lauren polo shirt had replaced the "Grateful Dead" and other rock' n' roll shirts he wore just a few months back. He was slow to answer questions and his speech was slightly slurred. *Telltale signs,* I thought to myself, *of his years of abuse.* Off drugs and alcohol for several months, John, sixteen years old and a junior in high school, now speaks against abuse before junior high groups. When he speaks, he begins with this confession: "I'm John and I'm a drug addict and an alcoholic." Although those very same words show up in almost every antidrug docudrama, I sensed that for John it isn't simply a canned phrase. I heard sincerity as he outlined his years of abuse. His story, he told me, is one of being there and back—and very glad to be back:

My problem really started with my attitude toward school and then it just crept into every other area of my life. I didn't care about anything—period. The only thing I really cared about was not hurting my drug-using friends. And as I think back, those were the people who hurt me the most during my drug and alcohol abuse. It didn't really bother me that I was hurting my parents through my abuse. Oh, I guess I did feel real guilty at first for always having to lie to my parents about drinking and using drugs. But before long, the guilt just turned to anger toward them. I used to always yell, "You don't understand me!" There were many times when I would even swear at my mom.

A few months back things just got too bad and I was sent to a treatment center. While I went into treatment against my will, I came out determined to keep sober and straight. I've had to fight real hard to get where I am now. But I also feel better than I ever have.

I have been off the stuff now nine months. I want a year real bad. It's just something I need to do for myself. Also, a lot of adults don't give kids any respect in the AA program until after they've been off a year. See, kids just come and go, come and go. For me, staying sober and straight is something I just have to prove I can do. There are certain things I set before me and I say, "Once I do this, I'll feel better about things." So far, I'm real happy with my progress.

One of the hardest things, apart from just the alcoholism and addiction itself, has been coming back home and facing my old friends. After I got back from the treatment center, I caught all kinds of flak for wanting to stay sober. It went all around the school that I was keeping straight. I had been one of the biggest partying guys here. It was like if you wanted to party with John, you were cool. Then it ended up like I was the biggest loser in school, at least in the eyes of my old drug-using friends. I see them in the halls, and they treat me like s——, to be real honest. They treat me real crappy, and it's hard. Kids who have been in treatment and have tried to get sober and didn't make it, they're the worst. They give me the most problems. I get called a narc a lot, even though I'm not one. My old girlfriend doesn't want anything to do with me, either.

Although I think they're wrong, I can see where they're coming from. When I came back after treatment, I had to look around and say, "Wow, I've never been in this school without partying." The longer I stayed sober and straight, the more I realized that everybody doesn't party. There are normal people who don't do drugs and alcohol. While before, I thought that everybody did it.

I have also had to give up more than just my old friends. For about two and a half months after treatment, I continued to wear my old concert T-shirts and I hardly ever shaved. I finally decided it was time for an image change. I got a haircut and started dressing nicer and stuff. It was hard for me to do that because that change was a big statement saying, "I'm not the same person." Other people, including teachers, were still expecting the same old person, however. I have remained determined to keep this change no matter what, because it's just important to me personally. But it still hurts a lot that others won't accept the change.

The gym teachers are the worst. They just refuse to admit that I'm not the person I was a year ago. They give me a lot of abuse, because I gave them a lot of s——, granted. But I've apologized to every *teacher in this school that I've ever given any hassles. It's been sincere. Sincerity is important to me now that I am sober and straight. I now have a lot of morals about what I should be as a person. There is a lot that I have had to change: my attitudes, the way I act in certain situations, the way I treat people, and the way I expect to be treated. People could walk all over me and it didn't really bother me much on the outside. I'd just let it go. Now I expect a little back.*

I'd like to just give this advice. Don't start drugs or alcohol. There are ways to keep from getting into the stuff. If the kids you hang around with are going to use and you don't want to, go somewhere else. There is always somebody else who is going to like you for who you are, and not for what you do. That's the hardest thing I've had to come to grips with this year. And while I still get some hassles, a lot of people—including some teachers—do like me for who I am, and that's hard to believe a lot of the time.

Amber: "I Wouldn't Call Myself a Winner Two Years Ago"

At sixteen, Amber is a realist. Maybe too much so. She looks at the world harshly, seeing many things such as her own alcoholism; her alcoholic father, now dead because of an alcohol-related car crash; her tense, cold relationship with her mother; and "outsiders" who seem unable to understand her or help her through her pain. But beyond the harshness that crept in through her speech and in the tiredness etched across her face, I saw an attractive girl dressed in fringed denim boots and jacket who was struggling hard to be a winner against abuse. And for the past year and three months, she has been winning. During our conversation, she stared hard and intently into my eyes as she said, "At first, you have to take it day by day. In the past several months, I haven't thought about alcohol that much unless I'm having a crisis. Then I think maybe I should go out and get drunk, but I know how that has affected me in the past and I know that it won't solve anything, so I don't do it. I'm never going to have control over alcohol, but I can be in control of my life."

The journey to that realization, however, has been far from easy:

I was in junior high when a boyfriend introduced me to pot. I was having a lot of family problems and when I got high with him, nothing mattered. So I just kept getting high on pot, and then I started drinking. When I drank, everything bad in my life would go away. Alcohol made me feel better. But when I came back to reality everything was worse. So I drank more. It was a vicious cycle. I was eventually admitted into a hospital for depression due to alcoholism. I got out of there and went back to drinking. Then a couple of years later, I was admitted into a treatment center. From there I went on to another hospital, then to a halfway house. This pattern went on for about ten months. During that time, something changed in me. I have now been sober for fifteen months.

Being addicted to drugs and alcohol has affected me a lot. I've lost many good friends because I was so into drugs that nothing else mattered. I put my [drug] use first and then everything else came after that.

I think one of the toughest things I have to handle right now is the attitude of nonusers. I really don't get along with people unless they are using drugs or recovering. People who have never used drugs don't understand me at all. They don't understand why I used drugs. They don't understand why I have to go to AA meetings. They don't understand why I couldn't just quit. But a person who uses knows what it's like and how it feels. Now, understand, I don't compromise with these people. I associate with them in school, but I don't go out with them, and I don't call them on the phone. I don't make plans with them and I don't go out with them on weekends. I know that would mean real trouble for me.

Although I don't compromise with abusers, I also don't preach at them. But I am willing to help them if they want help. I basically say that they can do what they want, but if they need help or want to talk to me, or if they feel like they're coming down, I'll be there for them. But I can't hold their hands and tell them what to do all the time. I could tell them, "Drugs are bad for you," but I wouldn't be the first person to say that. And it's not like they don't already know it, because it's obvious. You'd have to be a hermit to think that drugs aren't bad for you. They teach it to you in school, they show it to you on TV, and people just don't believe it. But I've been there, and I know I can't make them believe drugs and alcohol are dangerous. They have to see it for themselves. I'm the type of person who somebody could tell that the chair in the other room is green and I wouldn't believe them unless I went in there and saw it for myself. Maybe it's because I don't trust people that much. I only trust my own judgment. I think a lot of abusers are like that. And that may be why it's so hard to change them.

Of course, there are some users who do really get on my nerves: the braggers. When I hear them carrying on, I think cynically, Good for you. *Maybe I should be going up to them and trying to help them, but I know that if that were me I wouldn't want anyone getting into my business. But I just feel they're losers and they have a long way to go and a lot to learn. They're not winners for sure; I sure wouldn't have called myself a winner two years ago.*

Jeremy: "Drug Use Was a Real Power Kick"

With his long, wavy black hair, olive-colored skin, and tall, well-built frame, Jeremy could pass for a long-distance runner from the early Greek Olympics. He also has a personality that's easy to like. Open, friendly, talkative, his smile rarely leaves his face. About his abuse, the eighteen-year-old senior said, "It was always the search for the ultimate high. That's where any user lies to himself; from day one of use he'll never have such a high again. It's like a drug addict's body is geared to getting high, to feeling good. Whatever makes me feel good is what I'm going to do excessively."

For Jeremy, that obsession continues—but he has chosen to give it over to other less dangerous things, like eating junk food and attending AA meetings:

My dad is an alcoholic. My own personal belief is that I was destined for addiction. When that would happen or whatever would trigger it, was simply a coincidence. I'm not saying I blame my own problem on my dad's drinking. But I just believe that I have a predisposition to-ward addiction or abuse of some sort. So the addictive personality, the compulsion, was always there inside of me. Call it genetic or learned, but it was always around. What I chose to get into to satisfy that compulsion was not something healthy, like sports or academics, but drugs. The most destructive thing I could find.

When I got into drugs, I became an immediate daily user. I used pot, alcohol, acid, and cocaine on a daily basis. Sometimes I'd get high twelve or thirteen times a day. It was definitely problem city. I was a disaster waiting to happen. And it did happen. In October of '85 I went into treatment after being arrested for possession, vandal-ism, and reckless driving.

I was in treatment for seven weeks. In-patient counseling, the way I see it, was essential for breaking down all the walls I had built up for so long. When you're using drugs for a significant amount of time— alcohol as well, but more so drugs—you're emotionally stunted. I started using when I was fourteen and ended when I was seventeen. Emotionally, the way I deal with things right now, I'm still fourteen. It's like drugs put me in a timeless vacuum.

Through treatment I learned a lot about myself. I discovered I wasn't the best in the world; I wasn't the head honcho anymore. I learned that Jeremy could be wrong a lot of the time, that there were other things greater than myself. Drugs, I discovered, had really been a big ego trip. Obviously, drugs affect people differently, but for me it was a real power kick. Even today I still get off on being the one in control, having people come to me and saying, "Jeremy, we need you to do something for us." I have always needed to be in the spot-light. I get a high out of that. In the past I got my ego requirements taken care of through drugs. Today that high comes from speaking in groups, and helping a kid who's in trouble.

If I could say one thing to my peers and kids a bit younger, I'd say, "Running away is not going to get you anywhere. When you finally decide to come back home, you're going to be right where you left off. Running away is not the answer. Escape isn't healthy." My advice doesn't really carry much weight unless people really feel their prob-lem and are looking for it. But for those who would really listen and learn, I'd say, "Don't run away. Understand that to deal with the problem is the only healthy thing to do. Learn to be honest with your-self. Talk out your problems with other people. Don't internalize them."

FOUR

THE ROLES WE PLAY

WHERE DO YOU FIT IN?

After spending hours listening to and reading teenagers' widely varied thoughts on the drug and alcohol issue, I realized something: Each of us, adult and teenager, is somehow involved. Even those of us who don't drink or use any kind of drug are a part of the drug and alcohol problem in our own communities and schools. The role of users, of course, is obvious; nonusers' roles are not so obvious. Yet the concern or lack of concern of nonusers has a direct effect on the way a school or community goes about handling abusive situations.

With this in mind, I have developed four composite role pictures or stages. While none of us fits neatly under a given "sketch," I believe we each closely identify with one of these four types: active abuser, struggling abuser, bystander, problem solver. These types will be referred to frequently throughout the remainder of this book, and it is my hope that all of us will come closer to the character and posture of the last type: the problem solver.

TYPE #1: ACTIVE ABUSERS

According to the stereotype, active abusers are consumed by their use. They brag about it, know all the names for street drugs, hang around fellow drug abusers. They disrupt class and are frequently absent or in detention. They are rebels, rabble rousers, constantly fighting. Active abusers are living labels: dirtball, druggie, rocker, partier.

But our labels and stereotypes may be wrong. The active abusers may be quite friendly, or shy, or involved with sports, or studious. They may look like happy-go-lucky social drinkers. They may or may not be addicts or alcoholics. They certainly *do* have a problem, because for active abusers, fun is defined almost solely by the use of drugs or by the consumption of alcohol. Here are a few of the traits I have observed in active abusers:

"It's nobody else's business." Active abusers often are consumed with a sense of personal rights. They feel nobody has a right to tell them what to do. A seventeen-year-old guy from California commented: "I enjoy getting buzzed on alcohol and I don't see anything wrong with it, unless I endanger another person's life. I enjoy it or I probably wouldn't do it. It's none of the school's business what students do. It's the person's own life to do with as he wants." Since active abusers believe use is an individual choice, they will not become involved in trying to monitor a friend's overuse even if that friend has been close to overdose or death several times.

"As long as I don't hurt anybody." Active abusers often see their habit on a purely personal level, feeling that what they do affects nobody else. One girl from Arizona said, "You use responsibly if you just get stoned at home." Another person said, "I do drugs occasionally. I smoke marijuana and I drink. I've taken acid (LSD) once and I enjoyed it, but I wouldn't do it again: LSD is too unpredictable. I'm not saying that doing drugs is right, but as long as I don't let them take over my life, or my drinking doesn't hurt anyone, then why not? It's the choice of the user."

"It's not a problem." Active abusers refuse to admit that what they're doing is a problem. The possibility of addiction or alcoholism is not an issue for active abusers. The active user of street drugs may even show a good bit of pride in his abuse, displaying his status through wearing concert T-shirts, for instance. The drinking jock, on the other hand, may demonstrate his pride in abuse by bragging about the case of beer he downed on Saturday night, emphasizing his ability to hold his booze. (An "ability" that can be a sign of alcoholism.)

While the people around active abusers may see a pattern of severe problems, the abusers themselves seem oblivious to their destructive behavior. When asked to define the alcohol problem, a fifteen-year-old girl from Ohio responded simply, "There isn't one." A fifteen-year-old guy from Illinois, who claims to use marijuana, alcohol, mushrooms, LSD, and coke, said, "I feel drugs do not hurt anyone unless you get carried away with them or you can't handle them. The best way to know if I can handle it is, I usually quit three times a year for a few months. If I can't handle it I know I have a problem. But in the five years I have been doing drugs, I have never been addicted. What people do with their lives is none of your business." The inconsistency in his argument notwithstanding (quitting for a few months three times a year wouldn't give much time for use), this active abuser seems unaware that addiction is only one of the long-term negatives of prolonged abuse.

They seem defensive. Active abusers often are belligerent when confronted about the use of drugs. When asked about the drug problem, one person said quite pointedly, "Some people smoke weed *big s——!*" Active abusers scoff at the idea that peer pressure causes abuse, claiming they drink or use because "it tastes good," "I love the buzz," or "for the h—— of it."

They have personal problems. An inability to relate to peers, family problems, a family history of alcohol abuse, lack of self-worth, suicidal tendencies, or any number of problems may lie at the root of the active abusers' experiences.

Long-term abuse will most likely result in some of the following physical problems: addiction, lung disease, impaired memory (from marijuana use), use-related driving deaths, and injuries.

TYPE #2: STRUGGLING ABUSERS

When I met Mike out in front of his high school he had on a Coors jacket. Despite his open display of his favorite beer, Mike is restless about his use of alcohol and drugs. He lost a brother because of cocaine and now he fears the same fate might follow him. So he stays away from most drugs. But not alcohol. He sometimes likes to drink to escape the pain he feels from his brother's death. His drinking just causes more pain, however. He has been stopped many times for driving while intoxicated. One time he was clocked at 120 m.p.h. when four police cars finally stopped him. As a result of that experience, he vowed to cut down on his drinking. Now he only drinks on weekends instead of every night. Mike is a struggling abuser. He fears he may be an alcoholic. He realizes he has a problem but he is unable to do anything about it.

Struggling abusers may use daily or frequently (on weekends, for example). Unlike active abusers, struggling abusers are aware and willing to admit that a problem exists. While this admission is the first step to changing destructive behavior, strugglers feel paralyzed—unable to do anything about their habits. Like active abusers, struggling abusers may or may not be addicted to drugs or alcohol. Yet, regardless of whether or not the disease of addiction is present, these people do have a drinking or drug problem. Struggling abusers often display some or all of these characteristics:

They are aware of their own weaknesses but feel trapped, unable to change. A sixteen-year-old girl from Illinois who claimed she was just a social drinker said, "In the back of my head, I know drinking is a terrible habit. But it never occurs to me at the time I'm drinking to stop."

They feel torn between drinking and personal values. "I drink mainly because my friends do and we usually have fun," a seventeen-year-old girl from Iowa said. "I hate to drink, because I know it's wrong and I usually end up getting into trouble. I can't stop because I've tried. I don't drink a lot—I average once every two weeks, if even that."

The feelings of frustration over compromise are especially intense for the struggling abuser with religious sensitivity. One such individual wrote me to say: "I had been drinking for a while and finally decided it was really wrong. I had a big turnaround at that time. I even got baptized at church. Then, just three and a half months later, I got drunk. I lost a lot because of that: my sense of self-worth, the perspective of my religious convictions, confidence in myself, and my virginity.

"All of this, however, did not scare me off, but instead opened me up to about ten months of drinking, casual sex, and major changes in my morals. Well, maybe my morals didn't change but drinking seems to make me forget them temporarily.

"So far I have tried to quit four times, and now I am on my fifth try. It has only been a little over six weeks of no drinking, so I'm not sure if it's gonna last. But this time seems to be different. I hope so."

It should be noted that in certain situations, quitting on one's own is not possible. No matter how much the abuser desires to quit, no matter how strong the religious convictions, simply "gutting it out for God" does not work. This is especially true for the person who is not merely a problem drinker or drug abuser, but actually is an addict or an alcoholic. In this case, treatment for the disease of addiction must be sought before any changes can occur.[1]

They haven't thought through ways to refuse. Struggling abusers of-

---

[1]See Stephen Arterburn's *Growing Up Addicted,* (New York: Ballantine/ Epiphany, 1987) for further insight into this discussion.

ten go with the flow. They haven't given much thought to how they should respond to a particular situation. It may never have occurred to them that they could simply refuse. A sixteen-year-old girl from California said, "Teenagers sometimes don't know how to say no, which is a problem."

They fear the consequences of refusing. While some abusers may know how to refuse, they are afraid that refusal will get them tossed out of the in-crowd. According to the *Campus Life* surveys and many other reports measuring the power of peer influence, loss of friends, status, or popularity are major factors that keep teenagers from refusing to drink or use drugs. A seventeen-year-old girl commented: "I know it is not right to drink and it sounds like a cop-out to say I do it because my friends do. I do it only around friends and at parties. It's like you can't go anywhere without running into alcohol or drugs."

They are highly aware of and sensitive about the labels placed on abusers. "I stopped using cocaine," said a sixteen-year-old girl from Illinois, "because I hated being called a stupid idiot. So now I just get high on marijuana." The label helped this girl stop using cocaine. But in other situations labels such as "stupid idiot," "dirtball," and "druggie" simply reinforce strong feelings of low self-image.

They are aware of the pain abuse causes. Struggling abusers may have alcoholic parents, relatives who are addicted, or friends who died or were injured through alcohol-related accidents. If nothing else, the struggling abuser is incredibly in tune with personal pain. One struggler said: "The last time I drank I got so drunk that I didn't know where I was, and honestly didn't care. I look back on that with chills up my spine. I don't know what would have happened if I had been driving. I was upset, very upset. I ended up with bruises up and down my arms and a small one along my jaw from having my head on the toilet. I would be a hypocrite if I said I'd never drink again. But next time, I hope, I'll be a little older and more in control. Drinking has made me totally senseless. I couldn't tell you the number of times I passed out or threw up."

Sadly, a tragic background and bad experiences do not offer solutions; they only add to the struggler's frustration and feelings that he is unable to quit. An eighteen-year-old guy from Illinois said: "I can see drugs and alcohol are ruining friends and family, but it's hard to stop."

They are afraid to tell others. Teenagers have powerful fears that parents will not understand their problems. One girl who wrote me her story of alcohol abuse began by saying, "I have hastily written this. It is 1:30 a.m., and I am not about to rewrite it. I have to send it before my mother gets hold of it. You see, I have hopefully stopped drinking. And if my mother found out that I ever drank, heaven help me!" The girl then went on to outline a pattern of long-term abuse.

Fear—of punishment, of disappointing others, of ruining one's reputation—keeps teenagers (and adults) from revealing abuse. And what makes the problem worse is that parents often deny what they see. While parents aren't ignorant of society's drug and alcohol problem, they do not want to believe it affects their own families. So they refuse to believe the obvious.

They tend to send out signals. While struggling abusers may not come right out and say they abuse drugs or alcohol, they often offer hints that they feel trapped. I have italicized some of these signs in the following comment from a fifteen-year-old guy:

"I use drugs; I got started by my friends. I *periodically quit,* like the one time I got a bad buzz, and I *got scared.* But I still do drugs anyway. *Hopefully,* soon I will *stop.* But I don't worry, 'cause I have good willpower and can take care of myself. *Drinking has gotten me into trouble.* I have been to the police station already for drinking, but I know I can stop too! Cause my *dad is an alcoholic,* and I know how they act. I'm just a kid experimenting with different stuff. And soon I will stop *(hopefully)."*

They feel guilty most of the time. Hiding the abuse, breaking family or school rules, forsaking religious and personal convictions, causing pain to oneself and to others—all of this adds up to tremendous feelings of guilt and self-defeat.

They will warn others about the dangers of abuse. Because struggling abusers know the pain abuse causes, they often will tell others to stay away from it. One nonabuser wrote: "My friends who use drugs and alcohol tell me never to get into it."

TYPE #3: BYSTANDERS

Bystanders don't drink (or they drink very rarely) and don't use drugs. They usually stay clear of people who use drugs or drink alcohol. For the most part they just stand by. They are not involved in creating the problem, yet they also feel no obligation to contribute to the solution. Drug education materials often refer to bystanders as "enablers." By ignoring or denying the problem, they "enable" active abusers and struggling abusers to continue or even increase use. Thus bystanders, in a very real sense, *are* involved in perpetuating the problem of abuse. Here are some of the traits often seen in bystanders:

They either offer simplistic reasons as to why abusers use or they say they have no idea why abusers use.

When asked why students use drugs or drink, some say:

"I think using drugs is totally stupid. I mean, what's the use? Get high and then get hurt or killed. It's stupid. I think people only do it to get attention or to try and be stupidly cool" (Male, 15, Illinois).

"I don't know, they're stupid" (Male, 18, Michigan).

"I have no idea" (Female, 17, Washington).

"Abusers are just losers playing with their lives" (Male, 15, Michigan).

Bystanders often consider peer pressure a lame excuse. A fifteen-year-old guy from Illinois wrote: "People talk about peer pressure, but that's nonsense. No matter how much someone pressures you, if you don't want to do things, you won't." Unfortunately, people who don't understand the causes behind abuse or who feel drug users are simply too stupid to know better won't seek out constructive solutions.

They offer simplistic solutions. Bystanders will say things like, "They need to get their lives straightened out," "They need to stop," or "They should just be sent to detention when caught." The religious bystander may simply say, "They need to go to God for help." It's true that spiritual advice and religious perspective should play an important part in helping abusers, but religious bystanders are not really interested in solving the problem. They are simply satisfied with making simplistic religious pronouncements in lieu of becoming personally involved.

"It's a personal choice." Like active abusers, bystanders remain private about their opinions, wanting the abuser to do the same:

"It is my choice not to drink. I don't preach to other people about it. Let them make their own mistakes and decisions" (Female, 17, Texas).

"I don't say anything to any user, because I believe it's his life" (Female, 17, Missouri).

"If you want to use drugs and alcohol, fine, but keep the h—— away from me!" (Male, 17, Washington).

They can't relate. Bystanders may have little or no understanding about how people could ever get trapped in abuse. Like this fourteen-year-old from Missouri, bystanders do not understand the disease of alcoholism or addiction: "I can't understand how people could get addicted to drugs or alcohol when they've seen and have been told what will happen to them." Bystanders also are unable to empathize with some of the other root causes—such as family problems, peer pressure, or low self-esteem—that may bring about abuse.

They express either an uninformed paranoia or total disgust over all the fuss. Bystanders may believe that one drink causes alcoholism or smoking one marijuana cigarette causes brain damage. They may also feel that the problem is just too severe for them to be able to do anything about it. They feel inconsequential and overwhelmed, believing that there is no way they could make a difference. On the other hand, bystanders may just be tired of all the attention given to what they consider a minor problem. Disgust over the issue may lead a bystander to become calloused and insensitive. A sixteen-year-old guy from Washington, D.C., remarked: "I couldn't tell you why people use drugs, because I don't care about drugs or the users." Whether paranoia or disgust sums up bystanders' feelings, the bottom line is that this type of person just wants to stay away from abusers and their problems.

TYPE #4: PROBLEM SOLVERS

When I met Adam, now a college student, I couldn't help but be impressed with his stand. He had drive, initiative, and a creative plan for carrying out his solution to the drug and alcohol problem in his school. He set up a program called "Safe Rides" to help cut down on teenage drunken-driving accidents. Through his speeches and one-on-one contacts, many other kids caught the vision for "Safe Rides" and volunteered to give drunken teenagers and their passengers a safe ride home on the weekends. As an editor for his student newspaper, Adam wrote editorials about the drinking and drug problem in the school, and confronted school administrators for their complacency, denial, and lack of concern in solving the drug and alcohol problem. He also became the chief investigative journalist in a case involving a bar selling drinks to minors. His writing on the matter received national attention and helped focus greater concern on teenage drinking. His editorials and other writings went beyond only criticizing; they also presented solutions. Adam searched hard for creative ways to curtail the problem at his school and community.

What is Adam's reasoning for being such an activist? "St. Paul said that once you make that commitment to Jesus, the good works follow. And I've just wanted to be able to reach out both to my peers and to my community in very practical ways. I wanted to demonstrate that there's more to being a Christian than going to church on Sunday.

"I think the quote that I had put with my yearbook picture sums up why I do what I do: 'I would rather light a candle than curse the darkness.'"

Adam, of course, is a problem solver. This is not to say that all problem solvers are motivated by religious values. Nor must problem solvers do something major to help solve the problem of drug and alcohol abuse. There are little things, like a willingness to talk with peers about abuse, that can make a person a problem solver.

Consider the results of this *Campus Life* survey question: "Have you ever given advice to someone addicted to drugs or alcohol?":

As the statistics point out (see graph on next page), more than half of high school girls and about one-third of the high school guys are willing to offer advice to a person in need (the beginning stage of becoming a problem solver). It may not seem like a lot, but it is a beginning. If more students became involved in helping, and if more students had creative ways to help others solve their drug and drinking problems, and if more people had positive alternatives to offer, we would expect that statistic to rise dramatically. Those are big ifs, I know. But they are not impossible, as my experience with problem solvers shows, if more people will be willing to fit into this last type.

Here are some traits that characterize problem solvers:

They have healthy self-esteem, positive self-image. Individuals with a strong feeling of self-worth, who are self-sufficient and personally secure, are able to refuse drugs and alcohol. A seventeen-year-old female from Illinois comments: "I get high on life and I don't need chemical substances to be a part of the crowd." People with a good self-esteem are strong candidates for becoming problem solvers.

They are empathetic and caring toward the abuser. According to problem solvers, the abuser is a person who needs understanding and help, not some kind of stupid fool. A sixteen-year-old girl from Washington wrote: "People who use and abuse alcohol and drugs are not bad people. They need help, love, and understanding." Because of this, some of the best problem solvers are those who have had past problems with abuse. This, of course, does not mean that those who have never used should avoid involvement. Just the opposite. They have much to offer in terms of showing restraint and offering a positive example (and in promoting prevention programs). But if empathy isn't present, the would-be problem solver will simply come across as being a "goody-two-shoes" or as judgmental, and therefore will be ineffective.

GRAPH **17**

Have you ever given advice to someone addicted to drugs or alcohol?

YES   50%   100%

Male 36%

Female 55%

NO

Male 64%

Female 45%

What advice did you give?

"IT WILL RUIN YOUR LIFE"

18%

"YOU NEED TO GET HELP"

14%

"IT'S UNHEALTHY/DANGEROUS"

11%

"I CARE ABOUT YOU/I AM HERE TO LISTEN"

11%

Other advice included: "You Ought to Quit" ▪ "It's Not Right" ▪ "Drugs Are Stupid" ▪ "It's Me or Drugs" ▪ "You'll Lose Your Friends" ▪ "Do Other Things Instead" ▪ "Look at Yourself (See What a Mess You Are)"

Source: The 1986 *CAMPUS LIFE* survey of high school students.

How did the abuser respond to your advice?

"BRUSHED ME OFF"

38%

"NEGATIVE/ANGRY"

25%

"POSITIVELY"

21%

"IT TOOK TIME, BUT THE PERSON DID RESPOND POSITIVELY"

16%

Source: The 1986 *CAMPUS LIFE* survey of high school students.

They are educated and trained. Problem solvers know what they are talking about when it comes to drugs and alcohol. They don't just know the names of street drugs and various kinds of alcohol; they know the effects of those substances. They have often attended workshops and conferences, and have good, well-thought-out reasons why drug and alcohol abuse is to be avoided. Problem solvers often are trained in peer counseling. This does not make them professionals, but it does give them skills to help others in need and it gives them resources for finding professional help.

One sixteen-year-old guy who was involved in group peer counseling explained: "It takes a nudge to get most people going and, in my group, I'll give that nudge just to get them started. What I mean is that people will try to con you, lie to you. Since I have had my own drug problems in the past, I call their bluffs. They are surprised to find out that I know they are not being truthful. My little nudge to be more honest actually helps them open up more quickly." Problem solvers are good nudge givers.

They have a plan of action. Like Adam, problem solvers have a specific plan for improving the situation in their schools. Realizing there is power and greater creativity in numbers, they are willing to work with other students, teachers, and parents to improve on their ideas.

They are motivated by the needs they see. Because problem solvers are not involved in creating the problem, they can objectively see what drugs and alcohol are doing to their friends, school, and community. When I asked one sixteen-year-old problem solver why she is involved in fighting abuse, she said: "Because I see the need for it. I see people ruining their lives with drugs and alcohol. There aren't very many of my friends who don't drink. If there is a party most people are drinking— I'd say drinking more than the pot thing. When you go to a party it's very evident."

They see prevention as the key. Problem solvers feel that while rehabilitation is important, they must focus on preventing the problem from spreading. That's why they often challenge others to become involved in drug and alcohol free activities.

They focus on alternatives. Problem solvers do not simply say no, they offer alternatives to a drug and alcohol environment. Two girls I talked to from a Catholic school in Chicago have involved up to 300 students in a drug and alcohol free dance at their school. Students in a good number of other schools are offering activities that emphasize fun without substance abuse.

They have solid values and/or personal commitment to religious values. Like Adam, many problem solvers stress how religion motivates them to discuss drug problems with their friends. Their faith often leads them to become involved in long-term solutions. A sixteen-year-old girl who gives antidrug and antialcohol skits to elementary students remarked: "I don't think it works to be negative and hard on drug users. They get enough of that at home. Instead, I think Jesus gave a good example to follow. He ate with the tax collectors and other people who were considered bad, and gave them his positive example to follow. What he didn't do was say, 'You sinful, dirty people, why are you doing this?!' I think I get through to people best by setting a good example and showing them I care about them." If not Christians, problem solvers at least have strong personal values that motivate them to seek change.

They have a healthy view of community. People who are problem solvers do not say, "I don't care what you do, as long as it doesn't affect me." They believe we are all part of a community, not isolated individuals. That is, they believe that what each person does in some way affects or could affect another person. Therefore, a drug-using teenager (even if he claims to use only in his home) affects those around him in some way: family, friends, future family. Problem solvers believe everyone should be involved in constructive activities for the growth and enrichment of community life. Thus, problem solvers feel an obligation to help the abuser become a healthy contributor to society.

They realize they are not superhuman. I have given problem solvers some seemingly altruistic or self-sacrificing traits. However, a person who is a problem solver may not have all of the above traits. The person may just be someone who is willing to follow someone else's good ideas. But whether leading or following, problem solvers are active, if only in their small parts of the world. Problem solvers don't just stand by and watch a person or a school self-destruct. And while problem solvers cannot (and should not) take responsibility for others' actions or shortcomings, they try their best to make things better.

WHAT TYPE IS THE CASUAL DRINKER?

If a teen is a true "casual user" (see discussion in chapter 2), I would certainly not place him in either the "active abuser" or "struggling abuser" category. However, a word of caution is necessary: "Denial" is a natural part of any kind of abuse. So a person who would like to see himself as a casual user may actually be an abuser.

But suppose a teen really is a casual drinker, someone who drinks only rarely and does not get drunk. Could this person be a bystander? Yes. It's possible that the casual drinker may think, *Look, I don't have a problem, so why should anybody else?* It may be very hard for this person to empathize with and understand struggling or active abusers.

Could a teenage casual drinker fit in the "problem solver" category? It's possible. But in attempting to be a problem solver, teen casual drinkers also would be confronted by some real inconsistencies. They couldn't help but wonder, *Is my own drinking really right, since it is illegal and since I know the problems it can potentially cause?* Others will invariably see these incongruities, and that can only cancel out the chances for a teen casual drinker to be a role model for younger students. It would be easy for others to see this person as hypocritical and inconsistent. Several of the teens I talked with faulted fellow students for drinking while involved in certain drug and alcohol free groups.

Teens also face a "legal problem." If, for instance, a teen who is a casual drinker is picked up by the police for having a beer can in his hand, this person certainly undermines his claim as a problem solver.

The young person wanting to solve his school's alcohol and drug problem would do well to avoid even the "casual" appearance of alcohol consumption.

ADULTS: WHERE ARE THEY?

This book is about teenagers. Yet none of us lives, works, has fun, or goes to school in a vacuum. Adults—parents, teachers, administrators, coaches—affect the life of every teenager. So as I thought about the four different types of people, I wondered, *Where do adults fit in?* Like teenagers, adults fit into all stages in some way. However, there is one problem concerning adults that we need to focus on—a problem many teenagers are extremely and rightfully troubled over: adults' lack of awareness and their tendency toward denial. In other words, the problem of the adult bystander. Here are some comments from teens about this problem:

"Drug dependency is a problem at [name of school]. I'm not blaming the administration, but they sure are ignorant of it" (Male, 17, Iowa).

"Our administration says that our school does not have a drug problem. Either they know that there is a problem and just don't want to admit it, or they are totally blind and don't know what's going on around them" (Male, 15, Iowa).

"There is a lot more drinking and doing drugs going on than most parents and teachers want to believe!" (Female, 16, California).

"I don't feel adults realize how much drug and alcohol use/abuse is going on in teenage society. I'm sixteen years old and I haven't met more than three teenagers who can say they don't drink" (Female, 16, Wisconsin).

"It's so easy to hide from your parents. When you're high, you come home and you're laughing and acting silly and they think you're just being a teenager. You can come home stoned out of your head and they won't even know. A lot of parents don't want to believe it can happen to their kid. They think that's only on TV; it's true, every parent says that" (Female, 16, Colorado).

"We've recently had some pretty bad drinking situations at sporting events. After the teenagers leave, they drive under the influence. Some serious accidents have resulted. The teachers and administration are aware of these problems, but they haven't made many attempts to change them" (Female, 16, Michigan).

"Parents don't know their kid has a problem" (Female, 15, Oregon).

"Why is it that teachers and others in our community don't realize that drugs are a problem here?" (Female, 17, Michigan).

"Drug use here is denied by the administration. But there is a problem" (Male, 17, Iowa).

During the writing of this book I received a newspaper from a school in Virginia. The lead story in the newspaper outlined a drug survey that was recently conducted by that school's administrators. While indicating use and abuse a bit higher than some national studies, the survey results generally mirror national statistics on the use of drugs and alcohol. Commenting on the results, one administrator said that he felt the survey results were exaggerated. Maybe so. Maybe not.

Adam, the problem solver quoted earlier, found adult denial quite active when he confronted his school's drug and alcohol problem. Here, paraphrased from two days of conversations I had with Adam, are some of the problems he faced with adult denial:

I felt there was a need in my school for "Safe Rides," a teenage-run program that would keep teenagers from driving drunk or riding with a drunk. To get this going I knew I needed adult support, supervision, and financial backing. That was tough. With the exception of my parents and another family, I couldn't get adults involved. They were largely apathetic. And the principal of the school wasn't supportive; he just felt the problem wasn't bad enough. It was only after months of speaking engagements and personal phone calls that I had minimal adult support.

The same thing happened when I confronted the principal about the drug and alcohol problem we had right on school grounds. It was apparent we had a problem. Kids would go out and drink in their cars during school even with an on-duty policeman standing just outside the school doorway. Kids were smoking marijuana in the school restrooms. I knew; others knew. You could smell it. You could see the smoke. As the editor of the school newspaper, I started writing about the problems. I offered what I felt were some possible solutions. Among other things, I made this recommendation: If a teacher or an administrator suspects someone is smoking or drinking in the restroom, the policeman should be asked to come in and investigate the situation. The principal was outraged that I wrote this. He responded by saying the officer had no business coming inside the school, and, anyway, he said, the school doesn't have a problem.

At one point I even went so far as to grab the principal and take him into a restroom where some guys were smoking marijuana. Believe me, I didn't do this to be an informer. I did it out of concern and desperation. I wanted him to see how bad the problem was so he would do something about it. Instead, he walked in, chased the guys out and simply forgot about it. Just like nothing happened.

Yet, possibly the worst situation happened when I decided to investigate a bar that was selling to teenagers from my school and [from] a Catholic school down the street. On the afternoon before a Valentine's party was to take place at this bar, some high school students placed flyers on cars in the school parking lot. The flyers said, in large, bold print, 'Bar Available.' Some other reporters and I went there that night. An off-duty policeman was posted at the door. Students—minors—were drinking alcohol. I saw it.

The next day my story came out in the school newspaper that the bar was selling to minors, that minors were leaving and driving under the influence. You would have thought I had committed the crime. The principal got mad about my involvement, the local police chief labeled me and my fellow reporters "obnoxious," and stated that we had no business being involved in something that should have been left to the police. The fact that an off-duty policeman was hired to stand at the door made no difference to him. The local newspaper even sided with the police. I was clearly in the wrong, according to most adult decision makers involved.

Adam, who is from an affluent community in Connecticut, was eventually praised for his investigative work in a governor-supported editorial that appeared in the *Hartford Courant*. He also won first place for his investigative writing in the *Courant's* statewide journalism competition. All along he had the support of his parents and of people from his church, but until the situation was a statewide issue, other adults continued to deny the problem. And this may still be happening. On a visit to Adam's school a couple of years after the incident, I watched as kids came and went from cars in the parking lot during school hours. Posted in front of the school was an off-duty police officer.

Why this adult denial? Is it community politics—the fear of busting the superintendent's kid? Or that people don't want to stir up trouble? Or maybe some feeling that it couldn't happen in this nice little community? Or is it just plain hypocrisy?

What about on an individual family level? Why, for instance, will parents go for months, even years, without recognizing or admitting that their teenage child has a problem with drugs or alcohol? Is it fear that the family will fall apart if the problem is discovered or are parents simply naive? Or do they simply feel there's no need to get worked up about their own kid's use? These are tough questions. An entire book could and probably should explore them. But I will only say that like the teenage bystander, adult bystanders must be educated, they must admit problems, they must put aside politics—they *must* become involved if the problem is to be solved.

FRIENDSHIP: THE FIRST STEP
TO BECOMING A PROBLEM SOLVER

In my interactions with alcohol and drug abusers, I have found that many times even the active abusers are looking for help. Sometimes the best way to give that help is just to be a friend. I close this chapter with a challenge from a struggling abuser who lives in Chicago:

> *I started drugs in the seventh grade and I've been doing them for the past six years. I've done coke, marijuana, uppers, downers, alcohol, the whole bit. I lost my virginity one night when I was smashed. I can't remember those parties very well or things that went on at them; my friends have to tell me. Get this: my folks don't even know any of this.*
>
> *I've gone to school, school events (and this is a private school), work, church, concerts totally smashed. In school I never had caring friends. Even now I don't. I mostly hang around by myself or with people from the local public school. I've called myself a Christian for a long time, but deep down I know I'm not. Summertime is prime time for parties. I wish I could've remembered the summers of '84 and '85*

and '86. But I don't because I was too smashed to remember my name. If anyone who reads this is doing drugs or thinking about drugs and has a friend or friends that really care, go to those friends and ask them for help. I never did and I almost died from drugs, *but God gave me a second chance. I know there's a God and I hope someday I find him to thank him. I'm not quite free yet, I still drink and smoke pot, but someday . . . well, there might not be a someday for me.*

PART TWO

THE RESULTS OF DRUG AND ALCOHOL ABUSE

FIVE

HOW DRUGS AND ALCOHOL AFFECT THE INDIVIDUAL

*"It's nobody's d—— business who uses and who doesn't. As long as
people use drugs in their own home and aren't putting others in danger,
there isn't anything that the law should do to stop the drug user" (Female, 16, Texas).*

Is drug and alcohol use by teenagers an issue? Or is it only the user's
business? According to many teenagers, it is everyone's business because it affects everyone. The results of drug and alcohol abuse make a
long list. Even those results that affect only the user inevitably touch the
lives of others. Following are some of the areas in a person's life that are
affected by drug and alcohol abuse:

Disorientation and Incoherence
Students who regularly abuse drugs and alcohol lose track of time and
events. They have lapses in memory; some are unable to remember even
an entire summer. They also suffer loss of physical control and general
disorientation.

"Not remembering what I did was the worst, waking up the next day
and not remembering what I did. Not even one thing. I've had a few incidents where I went out into the public and was not even capable of
walking and it's really degrading. You don't remember it, but other peo-

ple tell you about it. Sometimes people would say, 'Don't you remember, you ended up with Rich or with Paul or somebody,' and you'd say, 'I don't remember.' You don't remember what you did with those guys. It blows your mind because you don't know what you did" (Female, 16, Colorado).

"I used to smoke pot all the time. I quit because it was impairing my ability to think" (Male, 15, Nevada).

Attitude and Personality

Anger and rebellion intensify in the abuser. An "I don't care" attitude is typical, and often is displayed through dress and grades. Drastic shifts in personality and mood swings are quite common.

"After doing crack for about three years my brother's personality changed drastically. His behavior was erratic. His good grades fell to pieces. He lied continually" (Male, 16, Washington).

"I have this one friend that I know who uses marijuana and he's still a very outgoing person, but in some things he has changed. Like you can tell he's becoming a little slower. His moods can really change now. He's not always as happy as he was" (Female, 18, Colorado).

"I don't take drugs and drink alcohol. I never plan to. I had friends who did and they have changed because of it. I don't like the change it makes in people!" (Female, 16, California).

"I quit using because I didn't like the attitude I was forming" (Male, 15, Idaho).

"I have a typical picture of a person with a drug problem: They usually wear combat-looking clothes, are on the wilder side, and are 'scummy.' Most druggies do poorly in school. They don't seem to care about anything: school, home life, or their appearance. People with drug problems stick out because of their 'I don't care' attitude" (Female, 16, Missouri).

"Before, when I was using a lot of drugs, I would just flip teachers the bird or something and just walk away. It didn't matter if they gave me a hard time. But now that I'm no longer using, it hits me real hard when a teacher calls me a burnout or something" (Male, 16, Illinois).

"You could be happy one minute—like everything's going right for you—and then you go off and get high with your friends and it just totally brings you down. I'm not just talking mentally, I'm talking physically too. I think you can tell when a person is getting high or drinking on the weekends by their attitude. For a teenager this is true. They get real jumpy and protective about certain things. Like if parents just ask a simple question, they get a real defensive response" (Female, 18, Colorado).

Self-Destruction
Because many users already suffer from a poor self-image, increased use tends to result in a self-destructive attitude. They see little reason for their existence and may attempt suicide.

"I almost committed suicide several times while I used" (Male, 16, Tennessee).

"My brother died using pills. It was suicide" (Male, 19, Colorado).

"While I was in treatment I overdosed on LSD and tried to commit suicide" (Female, 18, Illinois).

Schoolwork
People who abuse alcohol or drugs lose motivation for studies. Homework is left undone, grades drop, and teacher-student relationships erode.

"I told a friend of mine that smoking pot would make her grades drop, that she wouldn't want to do any homework. All she would want to do is smoke pot. So she went out and tried it and her grades dropped. She finally stopped and all her grades are OK now" (Male, 17, Washington).

"It affects their grades and their attitudes toward life. Most people smoke marijuana and it affects their grades in school and their family life with their parents—just the way they grow up and turn out. People who do it a lot are flunking out, so they don't have anything for a future" (Female, 18, Colorado).

"My drug counselors tell me that using drugs is how I got my F's. I kind of believe that. They tell me that I'm really quite bright" (Male, 17, Illinois).

"I know that when I was doing marijuana with my brother I noticed the difference in my grades. I wasn't comprehending what was being taught. I used for only two months. In the short span of time it was weird, because my grades started dropping. I know it was the pot. It's not like I used it all the time. Maybe every couple of weeks. I just hated that feeling of having my grades drop. I was doing so well at the beginning and I was so proud of myself" (Female, 16, Illinois).

"I was going to school and walking to class and a friend would say, 'Let's get stoned,' and so I would say, 'Sure,' and I would get stoned and go to class stoned out of my head. You don't even know what's going on. You can't remember half the stuff that you learned in class that day. You're doing so good in class and then the next day you can't remember anything you are supposed to know" (Female, 16, Colorado).

"Eleventh grade was when I was really bad. I had so many absences that it was pathetic. I'd rather ditch and go get high or be in trouble because of the drugs. It caused me a lot of trouble with teachers. I never went to school. I don't even know how I passed. Some drug users just sit there [in class] and act like they know what's going on, but they really don't. You go on thinking you made it that day, but when you go back the next day you can't remember being there yesterday" (Female, 18, Colorado).

The Probability of Increased Use

Drug and alcohol counselors talk about "gateway" drugs—drugs that lead to other drugs. The *Chicago Tribune* points out that cigarettes and alcohol are considered gateway drugs; they can lead to illicit drug use for many teenagers. Many drug specialists would also include marijuana as a gateway drug. While a good number of teenagers deny that the use of alcohol, cigarettes, and marijuana will lead to harder use, experience often says otherwise.

"In my drug using I was afraid of each drug before I tried it and then I finally said it didn't really matter. Pot and alcohol were OK, then I started downers, then I tried a little speed, then cocaine" (Male, 17, Illinois).

"Coke wasn't my main drug, pot was. But my experience with cocaine was a part of that continual search for the number one high. You get drunk and that's great, you have a great experience that first time. And then you drink some more, and you get drunk some more, and somehow it's not the same. So someone comes up to you and says, 'I've got this new drug, pot,' so you try pot and that's great too because it was the first time—it was new, it was different—but it's never the same again. So you keep going on that search for that number one high. You gotta keep trying new things in order for it to be the first time. So I tried coke. And coke was great the first time. But from then on it was simply satisfying what I once knew and it wasn't ever the first time again" (Male, 18, Illinois).

Disrupted Relationships

Many former users told me how drugs broke down friendships and family relationships. A sixteen-year-old girl from Nevada said: "I've lost my boyfriend because of alcohol and I've almost lost some friends." Even the occasional consumption of alcohol can create family problems and an overall breakdown in communication when users are "forced" to lie in order to hide their use.

Date Rape

According to Robert Coles and Geoffrey Stokes in their book *Sex and the American Teenager* (Harper & Row, New York, 1985): "Certain kinds of sexual activity and drug use are strongly related. Among teens who've used alcohol at all, almost half (47 percent) are nonvirgins; among those who haven't, 87 percent are virgins. For simply marijuana use, the association is similar, though not quite as high.

"A fourteen-year-old California boy was asked whether girls were 'easier' when they were high. He said: 'When they get high, it's kinda easier, 'cause they want to do stuff more. They won't go further, but they'll do the lesser stuff easier. But when they're drunk they don't know what they're doing.'"

Coles and Stokes did not use the term *date rape,* but I believe it is an appropriate term to use in the context of drug- and alcohol-related sexual encounters. Date rape takes place when a person is forced to perform a sex act against his or her will. When a teenage guy, for instance, gives a girl drugs or alcohol to "loosen" her up and get her to go along with sexual activity, I believe date rape has taken place. The victim is led to do something he or she would not do while not high or under the influence.

Near the end of my research for this book, I spent one morning talking to several teenagers who are involved in a drug education and counseling program in the Chicago suburbs. The first four teens quoted below are rehabilitated alcoholics or addicts or both. The last two have never used. I asked each of them this question: "Does a teenager give out drugs or alcohol to take sexual advantage of another person?" Here are their responses:

"Yeah, I can remember when I was younger a lot of people did that, especially when I'd go to parties downtown. They'd do stuff like slip a Mickey into our drinks. They would take advantage of us. But it's like, once you got on drugs you just changed into another person. You had no values, no morals, no nothing—you didn't care. Drug users will sleep with anybody. I can remember I was the same way. I never wanted to be that way, it was just what happened" (Female, 18).

"Yeah. I don't think it's the real bad users as much as maybe the sophomore kids on the football team. It's that kind of stereotype. The guys will get the girls to a party and get them drunk and have sex with them and stuff. It happens a lot. Sex didn't really matter to me. For the real heavy users, if they need sex they could just find a girl. There are girls who are just as trampy as the guys are. There are a lot of guys who are real trampy, they just want to go around and screw everybody. Me, I just wanted to get high. Sex could wait" (Male, 17).

"Oh, yeah. It happens a lot. I used to do it. I would get girls high and then hop in the sack" (Male, 18).

"I've never seen that. That never happened to me. I've never done it to anybody and it's never been done to me. I've seen it in the movies. Maybe it happens downtown on the south side of Chicago. But I don't live there so I don't know" (Female, 16).

"Yes. I've never been in a situation. I've never known of anyone who has been in the situation, but I've heard stories and I think they are true. I'm not saying it happens a lot, but I think it does happen" (Female, 15).

"Sometimes. It depends on the person. I know my freshman year someone tried to take advantage of me. They wanted to get me drunk and I said no. It was hilarious. It was the first freshman party. The first time I meet this guy, he says, 'Oh, I'm going to get you drunk so I can take advantage of you,' and I said, 'Boy, you blew your cover.' It depends if you are the kind of person that someone can push into doing something. If you're going to follow everybody else, then sure, it might lead to that" (Female, 16).

DEPENDENCY: THE CURSE OF ADDICTION

With increased use comes the distinct possibility of drug or alcohol addiction. The problems described above—problems with attitude, relationships, school attendance, and so on—probably affect more teenagers than does addiction or alcoholism. Many abusers are not, and will never be, addicts. Still, the curse of addiction devastates those it touches. And many teenagers are aware of this.

"Most people drink because it is fun, but then some of them can't stop" (Female, 15, Minnesota).

"I think people have a real problem when they can't go without their drugs for more than a couple of days" (Female, 16, Minnesota).

"When you become involved with drugs, you become dependent on them and they dictate what happens to your life" (Female, 17, South Carolina).

"I drink once in a while, but some teens seem to be totally obsessed by it. That's all they want to do, even on weeknights. Last year one of my friends had to go to AA, and another friend had to go to a drug rehabilitation center. That's scary" (Female, 16, Minnesota).

"A lot of people may say they're not addicted, but they are, even if it's pot. Even if they say they do it once a week or only on weekends, it doesn't matter when you do it, you do it. You need it" (Female, 16, Colorado).

"My parents used to worry about me a lot because I would just go out one day and I wouldn't come back for a few days. That whole time I would be drinking. When I was sixteen I would drink every day. I just craved it bad, so bad I could taste it in my mouth" (Female, 18, Colorado).

"I freebased [used the smokable form of cocaine] maybe once or twice and I really didn't like that. After a while I could tell I needed more and more to get the same high and that was scaring me. Then I started thinking that maybe I had a problem so I stopped doing cocaine and I moved on to LSD. You kind of switch; you don't say, 'I have a problem,' but 'I have a problem with a certain drug.' So you stop doing that and move on to another" (Female, 18, Chicago).

"When I first went into treatment, I couldn't stay straight a week" (Male, 17, Chicago).

"A lot of people take drinking as funny, you know. Like, 'Oh, my G——, so and so got drunk Friday night and it was really funny because he did a lot of stupid things.' People joke around with it. Others get more serious, though, and think, *This person drinks a lot. Maybe he'll become an alcoholic,* and they get worried. I worry about a lot of my friends" (Female, 16, Illinois).

"I think those TV commercials that show what happens to alcoholics are good. They just bring back too many bad memories. They show the commercial where they bring in the wagon and say, 'Many alcoholics get on the wagon—but this is the only wagon they'll ever stay on . . .' and then they show a casket, and that is one that really affects me. I know that I could have died from my alcoholism. I know people who I really care about and had relationships with, like my ex-boyfriend, who will probably end up getting killed or dying from alcoholism" (Female, 16, Chicago).

Addiction: Some Points of Explanation
Addictive behavior applies to virtually everything: cocaine, three-martini lunches, the need for that eighteenth cup of coffee (yes, caffeine is an

addictive drug), and even peanut butter binges. Psychologists refer to "addictive personalities," exploring such areas as unhealthy possessiveness in relationships. There is even an organization called Sex Addicts Anonymous.

One eighteen-year-old reformed drug addict from Chicago still appears to display addictive behavior: "Addiction applies to my life today, even after drugs. Like food. Food is a biggy. If I like something in particular I'll eat enough of it to make myself sick. It's disgusting. AA meetings—I can never go to enough of those. I was addicted to my girlfriend for a long time, thinking that as soon as I got with my girlfriend things were going to be great."

Whether this person's problem is a so-called addictive personality or simply the need to fill a hole the drugs left behind is hard to say. He believes, he told me, his past drug addiction is rooted in his personality—something he received genetically from his alcoholic father.

Nonetheless, drug addiction and alcoholism are quite distinct from other "addictive" behavior. I personally find a "peanut butter addiction," for instance, slightly humorous. And the boy quoted above told me that while his obsession with AA meetings may be an addiction, it is not a dangerous addiction as were his use of marijuana, cocaine, and alcohol. I heartily agree.

The Department of Education, an excellent and inexpensive resource for drug and alcohol abuse information, offers some important clarifications on drug and alcohol dependence:

Drugs cause physical and emotional dependence. Users may develop an overwhelming craving for specific drugs and their bodies may respond to the presence of drugs in ways that lead to increased use.

Regular users of drugs develop tolerance (the need to take larger doses to get the same initial effect). They may respond by combining drugs, which frequently has devastating results. Many teenage drug users calling national cocaine hot lines report that they take other drugs just to counteract the unpleasant effects of cocaine.

Certain drugs, such as opiates and barbiturates, create physical dependence. With prolonged use, these drugs become part of the body chemistry. When a regular user stops taking drugs the body experiences a physiological trauma known as *withdrawal.*

Psychological dependence occurs when drug taking becomes the center of the user's life. Psychological dependence erodes school performance and can destroy ties to family, friendships, outside interests, values, and goals. A person goes from taking drugs to feel good to taking them to keep from feeling bad. Over time, drug use itself heightens the bad feelings and can leave the user suicidal. More than half of all adolescent suicides are drug-related.

Drugs and their harmful side effects can remain in the body long after use has stopped. The extent to which a drug is retained in the body depends on the drug's chemical composition, that is, whether or not it is fat-soluble. Fat-soluble drugs such as marijuana, PCP, and LSD seek out and settle in the fatty tissues of the brain. Such accumulation of drugs and their slow release over time may cause delayed effects or flashbacks for weeks (and even months) after drug use has stopped.

BARBARA'S STORY: FROM THEORY TO REALITY

It's easy to get lost in theory. But Barbara's story, like many others, is far from theory. Instead, it shows the painful reality of addiction:

Many times I didn't want to use drugs and alcohol, but I forced myself so that my friends wouldn't make fun of me. I remember thinking that people wouldn't like me if I didn't do what they were doing. So I began taking more and more drugs.

Eventually I started liking the instant gratification I got from drugs. I didn't have to face my problems with school, with boys, with growing up. I didn't hurt as long as I had drugs. I was failing school, but my "druggie" friends were more important than my future or even my family.

I left home when I was seventeen to live in California with a drug dealer. I became a heroin addict at eighteen. The drug just swallowed me up. It became my obsession. I'd do anything for it. I started selling my possessions to buy heroin. When I had nothing left to pawn, I stole from friends and strangers.

My life was out of control. I never wanted to eat and I always felt like I had the flu. I'd have to drag myself out of bed in the mornings. I thought there was no way I could ever live like a normal person. I am different from other people, *I decided,* and I need drugs to feel normal.

But eventually the pain got so bad I thought I had to do something. So I tried very hard to quit. I cut back on my drug use until it hurt, until I couldn't stand the other pain—the pain of withdrawal. I cut out everything but the heroin. I thought if I limited my addiction to only one drug, I could gradually get off that one too. Instead, I simply used more heroin.

It was impossible to control the drug use; it controlled me. So I checked into a short-term treatment center. The staff tried to teach me that I needed a higher power for help, a power stronger than drugs. I thought the strongest power was heroin.

I left treatment determined to be straight, but that only lasted a short time. All it took was one exposure to drugs and I was off again, possessed by a craving I couldn't control. Six months later I was shooting up cocaine and heroin together, or "speedballing."

The worst day of my life was Christmas Eve, 1984. I enjoyed a delicious Christmas dinner with friends and had bought them presents. But after supper we got out the drugs as usual. One girl and I were preparing our syringes in the bathroom. The veins in her arms were so damaged that she couldn't find a place to inject her drugs. She stabbed her arms countless times trying to find an undamaged vein. Blood was all over the bathroom, running down the walls and in the sink. I could see myself in her; I knew I'd soon be the same way.

I injected my drugs, only to get an immediate craving for more. I threw up my dinner and ran out to find more drugs . . . on Christmas Eve! I hated myself so much! I wanted to overdose and die that night.

I had nothing left to lose but myself and at that point I didn't even care. Somehow, though, I had sense enough to go home to the only ones who still loved me. My family talked me into going to the Florida LIFE rehab center, a peer-oriented drug counseling program with a Christian emphasis.

After several weeks at this live-in center, the Christian message started sinking in. I did want help. But I still felt too mixed up, too confused, and too ashamed to share out loud. So I began praying silently during the group counseling sessions, hoping God would change my feelings and attitudes.

Eventually, I started opening up to the others and crying about the wrong things I'd done. As I shared my bad feelings, the desire for drugs faded. One day I realized that I did like myself again. I could look into the mirror without crying!

Even with counseling, and even with the help of God, the changes have come very slowly. Long-term drug treatment and prayer is the only combination that works when a life is as messed up as mine was. There is no quick fix when you're that far down.

ALCOHOL, ALCOHOLISM:
DIFFERENT, BUT THE SAME

Alcohol is a drug quite different from all others. Just the fact that it is so socially accepted makes it different. Also, the fact that it is "selectively addicting"—which, according to the experts, means some people are susceptible to alcoholism while others are not—makes it drastically different from many other drugs. If a parent has a tendency toward alcoholism there is a strong chance his children will inherit that tendency. And if abuse is present in a person's family, there is a good chance of that person abusing alcohol and other drugs. (Many of the teenagers I talked with who are reformed alcoholics have a parent or other family member who suffers from the disease of alcoholism.) Consider the comments of these rehabilitated alcoholics and addicts from the Chicago area:

"Everybody in my family except my mother has been touched with the disease of alcoholism. Nobody is really recovering except me and my grandma. Mostly everybody's an alcoholic in the family" (Female, 18).

"My dad is an alcoholic. My own personal belief is that I was destined to use. I was destined to at some point in my life" (Male, 18).

"When I was little, my real father died from a car accident related to his use of alcohol. Drug addiction and alcoholism were inevitable. My real father was an alcoholic" (Female, 16).

Project 714 (which is highlighted in chapter 7) is a student-run, high school-based program promoting a drug and alcohol free life-style. It offers the following useful list to check the possibility of dependency. According to the student leaders of Project 714, a "yes" answer to even a couple of the following questions could indicate a person has a serious problem and should seek help immediately.

Do you think about drugs or alcohol, or your next opportunity to use them, often?
Do you use chemicals before going to parties, or gulp drinks quickly to get a buzz?
Do you find that it takes more alcohol to get drunk or more chemical to get stoned than it used to?
Do you use alcohol or drugs to help you relax or go to sleep?
Do you drink or use chemicals frequently when you are alone?
Have you ever had difficulty remembering what happened the morning after drinking or using drugs?

Do you hide bottles or a stash somewhere "in case you need it?"
Do you find yourself drinking more than you have planned?
After a night of drinking or using chemicals, have you ever found your-
self unable to stop your hands or your whole body from shaking?
Do you drink or use drugs early in the morning to help you forget the
night before or to get over a hangover?

LIVING WITH ADDICTION IN THE FAMILY

The greatest influence in a teenager's life is the family. Whatever its
makeup, the family has a direct bearing on how adolescents feel about
drugs and alcohol. Sometimes having family members who are active or
struggling abusers causes teenagers to renounce use.

"My sister did drugs and it almost cost her her life; I hate drugs and
most people who do [them]" (Male, 16, Georgia).

"I don't drink because my father used to be an alcoholic, and we had a
lot of family problems, and he lost his job and wife. So I saw what it did
to him" (Male, 16, Illinois).

"My brother is an alcoholic and I don't want to end up like him" (Female, 15, Georgia).

"Someone in my family drinks and I see how terribly it affects him"
(Female, 14, Georgia).

"My step-dad is an alcoholic. I hate it because I had to see my mom
get beat up a lot. I think people with this problem definitely need a lot of
help. He's better now, but he is still lazy. He and Mom also smoke pot.
They have always argued and still do sometimes. When he is drunk, my
step-dad sometimes hits me and my half-brother when he fights with my
mom. He's a great guy and I love him. I am glad he's got this far"
(Female, 15, Michigan).

"My dad grows pot and smokes it a lot with all his friends. When my
parents were married, he'd come home really drunk and high and stuff
and beat my mom up. So my mom, my brother, and I moved to California. And I just recently moved up here to live with my dad. My mom
and dad got a divorce because of his habit. He beats my step-mom up
sometimes. When he comes home really high and stuff he's real edgy.
But he's been laying off a lot lately because he's been going to school.
But he still continues to smoke it. I don't smoke mainly because it
doesn't do anything for me" (Male, 17, Washington).

"I come from an alcoholic home and I know of the harsh realities that a drinker can bring into a home. You deal with the problems as a family unit, for all are affected" (Female, 16, Ohio).

"I don't drink. My dad drank and I saw what it did to him" (Female, 16, Georgia).

"I don't drink because my father is an alcoholic" (Female, 15, South Carolina).

"I have a family that has alcohol problems. It doesn't do any good for a marriage" (Male, 18, Oregon).

"My stepfather drinks and I would hate to become addicted to alcohol like he is" (Female, 16, Georgia).

"My sister started drinking in high school and almost ruined her life and my family" (Female, 15, Minnesota).

"My dad was an alcoholic and almost killed me in a car [accident]. I just don't want any of the problems he's had" (Female, 16, Missouri).

"My brother used to use them and I saw what it did to him. I never want to be like that, so I don't use drugs" (Female, 15, South Carolina).

"I have never been curious about using drugs. My uncle died from them, so they scare me" (Female, 16, Georgia).

"My friend's father is an alcoholic. He has been to rehabilitation centers several times, but he never seems to be cured. This is terrible. He comes home and yells at his wife and kids for no reason whatsoever. This situation is terrible. I pray for the man, and I get upset because he depresses my friend so much. Nothing my friend does seems right to the father.

"However, one day I was listening to my friend talk about his pain when it suddenly came to me: the good side. My friend has never had a drink of alcohol and never will because he can't bring onto himself what his father suffers. My friend will never make his future family suffer like this for him. My friend's future children and wife won't have to take uncontrollable verbal abuse like what his father dishes out. Because of his father, my friend is going to live a straight and sober life" (Female, 17, New Jersey).

THE OTHER SIDE OF AVERSION

In the cases above, teenagers demonstrate a strong aversion to drug and alcohol use because of what it does to the family. However, the above quotes hardly represent the rule. The substance abuse and addiction of a parent often lead to substance abuse and addiction of the teenager. It's a pattern that is hard to break and it's a pattern that has had long-term, disastrous results on the health of millions of families across America.

As pointed out before, alcoholic parents not only hurt themselves, but they also create unending pain for the entire family. What follows are two stories; the first one is a letter I received through the mail and the second is condensed from an interview. What is encouraging about both stories is that each teenager has been willing to seek professional help to handle her own feelings.

"I Thought It Was Normal To Drink"

I grew up with my parents drinking. I thought it was normal to drink all day and then fight all night. Yet eventually I began to realize my parents' behavior was quite different from the average family. I noticed my friends' parents did not go into the bathroom to take a drink like my parents did. But they drank in the living room or during dinner and rarely got drunk and fought. This was about the time I realized that alcohol was controlling my parents' lives as well as my own. I would fight with them. Then when we made up, I would pour their liquor for them, which only caused them to go out and buy more. I soon found that I was taking responsibility for their actions by making excuses for them, helping them cover up their habit.

They tried to get sober through different means: church, AA, etc. But when one would want to get sober, the other would fall off the wagon and pull the other one down too.

I began to go to Alateen[1] to find out how to get them sober. I soon found out that my parents were sick with the disease of alcoholism and that I could do nothing to get them sober. But I could work on myself and my actions and leave my parents to God.

A few years later, things did begin to change. But not in the way I had always hoped for. In 1974, my mother died of cirrhosis of the liver. My father still continued to drink. Two years later, I was put in a foster home for four months. During these four months, my dad joined AA and came to believe in a Power higher than himself. He finally got sober. After I came back home, I began to realize that he had changed, but I had not. I still had not yielded my life to God.

[1]Alateen and Adult Children of Alcoholics (ACOA) are support groups for children of alcoholics. Such support groups are located in many communities across the United States and can be found in the Yellow Pages or contacted through Alcoholics Anonymous. Help can also be found by calling the Al-Anon Family Groups at this toll free number: 1-800-356-9996. In New York and Canada, call 212-245-31ɔ1.

Needless to say, we fought a lot until I finally let Jesus reign in my life in 1982.

Even though Alateen is not a Christian organization, I found Christ in their love. They have always been there for me when I needed them, just like Jesus. So every day I thank my God and his Son for Alateen and pray that he will continue to use Alateen to help children who hurt from their parents' drinking.

"My Home Life Is Real Unpredictable"

During the interviews I had at the suburban Chicago high school mentioned earlier, I talked mostly with students who were rehabilitated drug addicts and alcoholics. Michelle's[2] case is different. Her stepfather had been an alcoholic for several years. Common to situations like Michelle's, her mother is a bystander (see chapter 4). Unlike her mother, Michelle is willing to admit that her stepfather is an alcoholic. According to experts in the field of alcoholism, Michelle's home life is quite similar to millions of others who live in homes where there is an alcoholic.

Home life is real unpredictable. My dad is an alcoholic. Well, he's not really my dad, he's my step-dad. He's more of a binge drinker than a constant day-to-day drinker. He married my mom when I was about four, so he's been an alcoholic at least thirteen years that I know of. On the surface, Dad looks like a success. He and Mom own a business that has always done quite well.

He admitted to me one time that he has a problem. About three months ago when he was drunk he said to me, "Do you think I have a drinking problem?" And I said, "Yes, do you?" He said, "I know I'm an alcoholic and there's nothing you can do about it." That hurt me but it also surprised me, because he was sort of sarcastic in the way that he said it. It was almost like he was saying, "To hell with you all, I'm going to do what I want to do. If I want to have my four-martini lunches with my business clients I'm going to do it."

My mother has enabled him to the point where it's really sick. Enabling means she covers up for him. I'll come home and say, "Where's Dad?" and she'll say, "He's upstairs sleeping. He's not feeling well." "Well, what's wrong with him?" I'll ask. She'll say, "Oh, he's sick," or "He's got a cold," or something like that. When in reality he's upstairs passed out or I can hear him retching in the bathroom.

[2]Not her real name.

My mother has never admitted that Dad is an alcoholic. I said to her one time, "He's got a drinking problem, Mom. You can't deny that he's got a definite drinking problem." And she said, "No, I don't think he does." So I said, "Well, why does he drink so much?" She said, "He likes the taste of alcohol." I said, "Oh, it's just the taste! That's why he drinks six martinis at lunch, comes home and has two before-dinner drinks, a few after dinner, and by eight o'clock we're sitting watching TV and he's passed out on the couch. He likes the taste—right!" And she just walked away from me. I don't know. My mom is not real open at all. I know she cares a lot about me and a lot about our family, but she wasn't brought up in an atmosphere where you share your feelings.

I love my mom a lot. I don't know what I feel toward my dad right now. I guess I want to feel sorry for him. It's so hard for me to accept that his drinking problem is the result of a disease. I think a lot of times I put a lot of blame on him that's not really his, like it's his fault this has happened. It's really not. He is sick and unable to stop. Six years ago he had to have open heart surgery and a double bypass. My dad's a big man, like Orson Welles, and they told him to quit drinking and to quit smoking and to cut down on what he eats. Well, he gave up smoking and he lost about fifty pounds, but he didn't give up drinking. He gave up drinking for about three months, but he went right back to it.

My brother alienates himself from my dad. My brother is twenty and lives at home. Basically, he wants nothing to do with Dad because whenever he deals with Dad at all, it ends up in a yelling match. It's never really dealing with the problem or talking things out. It's more surface-level things, like Dad telling him: "Don't forget to take out the garbage," or "Pull your motorcycle over closer to the side of the house." When my brother and my dad talk it's not really talking, even. My dad will shout at my brother to do something and he'll finally do it and that's the end of their "communication."

I'm really not close to my dad, either. I'll have to say that both my brother and I get along better with Mom than with Dad. The two of us are closer to Mom simply because the alcohol keeps us from getting close to Dad.

I went through a time when I couldn't decide if I liked him better sober or drunk. When drunk he's able to talk more freely and talk about things that normally never get talked about, like sex. But when he is sober he doesn't talk to me. I'm over that time now; his drinking is so destructive.

I know a lot of kids feel responsible for a parent's behavior. But I never have. I've always felt ashamed of it. I don't want anyone to see what a mess he can be. I'll always go home first and check out the scene before anyone comes over.

Holidays are always the pits. It's like the worst time in my house. Christmas at my house always winds up to be pretty bad. My dad ends up getting drunk, that's guaranteed, and something irrational will happen. It's just like you expect it every year.

One alcoholic affects about twenty-five people around him, at least. I know that I'm affected directly by this person. I have to see him every day. When I don't have to see him, it's great.

I started helping myself about a year ago by attending ACOA meetings, which stands for Adult Children of Alcoholics. By going I found I was really hurting inside. I lived with this guy who's supposed to be my dad, and I didn't want to live with him, and I hated him so much. In fact, I had gotten to the point where I wanted to alienate myself from my entire family. I hated them all. I never wanted to be home. The ACOA meetings helped me deal with a lot of these feelings of hatred and disgust. They taught me how to handle the situation better.

ACOA follows the same twelve steps that AA works on. But in ACOA, they're applied to you as a person who lives with an alcoholic. In ACOA we air our feelings or our experiences on a certain topic. Someone may say something that will trigger an experience I haven't thought about in maybe eight years. It may be about a childhood experience I had, maybe a real [bad] experience. And I can just relate to that and say, "I know how you feel when the alcoholic in your family did that to you. I had something very similar happen to me." Just to talk about that openly feels really good. It feels like you're sloughing off layers of yourself. It's almost like the alcoholic has frozen this heart of yours by his drinking, and you're kind of de-icing it by talking to others.

I had heard through ACOA that a lot of people in my situation have therapists, and I thought, Maybe I can speed up this process a little bit by going to one. *So I asked my boyfriend, himself a recovering addict and alcoholic, if he thought it would be good for me to see a therapist. He thought I should talk to my mom about it. I said, "Tell my mom I want to see a therapist? She would think I was nuts." I did manage to do it, however. And she said, "Why?" So I told her that there were a lot of things I didn't feel comfortable about, and that I would like to share them with someone who has a very unbiased opinion.*

So I started going to a therapist for a while. It helped me because I was able to talk about myself better. Then came the family sessions. We had two such sessions, which my brother never went to. My mom, my dad, and I went. It wound up with my dad being very much into denial. My mom and I were both crying the whole session and my dad was just like a rock. You couldn't even get to his feelings. They were very unsuccessful sessions.

I know that my dad's problem has affected my own attitude about drinking. About two years ago, I thought it was fine to go out and drink socially and get drunk on weekends. It was very acceptable among my peers. My older brother would have a party and all of our friends would be there. I would get drunk, all my friends would get drunk, everyone was drunk, and it was fun, you know. But after an evening like that the fun would go away and I would get very depressed. So I have decided to stop drinking. I'm not an alcoholic or an addict; I still feel I could drink socially but I just choose not to. I know that I am more susceptible to alcoholism because I live in the situation where it is present. I don't ever want to go through all the pain that an alcoholic or addict goes through, so I don't get involved with drugs either.

I have a lot of friends who are recovering addicts and alcoholics. Whenever they go out they never drink. They find other modes of having fun and doing things. It's kind of weird because I feel like I have two sets of friends—one set where it is socially acceptable to drink and do drugs and the other set who has learned to have fun without it.

At this point, I asked Michelle what advice she would give someone who lives with an alcoholic. She quickly asked in return, "Are they willing to seek help?"—something Michelle feels is essential for dealing with a problem situation. For those willing to seek help, she gives the following advice:

Pray. Then seek help. Before I started looking, I never knew there was so much help available. There are counselors, programs through the public schools, open AA meetings that anyone can attend, Alateen and ACOA groups for children of alcoholic parents, and special groups for spouses.

I guess I also would tell that person, "There are other people with problems just like yours, so don't give up, because if you give up you've lost the fight. You have to be strong. You can get strength through support groups." It was a lot of pain and a lot of tears for me. There is a lot of confusion and that's what causes the pain and the tears. But day by day I'm learning to deal with it through support groups and through friends who are real caring.

SURVIVAL SKILLS

Claudette K. McShane, a social worker and counselor in Milwaukee, Wisconsin, offered *Campus Life* magazine some insights on living with an alcoholic parent. Reprinted here are her helpful insights.

What can be done if you are currently living at home with an alcoholic parent? Here are some suggestions to help you on the road to normalcy:

Name the illness. *Say it out loud. "My parent is an alcoholic and I am the child of an alcoholic." This is the first step to recovering yourself and your lost childhood.*

Read. Get as much information as you can about alcoholism and being a child of an alcoholic. This will help you understand and trust your feelings about what is happening at home.

Disengage. Stay out of arguments with your parents, because it's a no-win situation.

Withdraw. Recognize the need to trust yourself and turn inward for the truth about what's happening. Your mind, and often other nonalcoholics in the family, will continually try to "trick" you into pretending that this is a "normal" family situation.

Pray and meditate. Don't turn inward alone. God understands your situation and is there to support you and love you. Talk to him about all your feelings: anger, frustration, loneliness, false guilt. Meditate on the Psalms and other passages from the Bible that offer comfort and words of encouragement.

Get support. Provide a context for understanding what's been happening in your life. Join Alateen or another support group for children of alcoholics. Find others who are experiencing the same things. It can give you strength and help build trust in yourself and your feelings.

Turn to the church. For the Christian support has two sides: professional help through groups like Alateen and spiritual help and guidance through a church. Find a pastor, youth worker, or some other mature Christian adult to talk to and pray with. This should be someone you can trust, someone who understands the disease of alcoholism, someone you can call when things get too tough at home. Also, seek out others in your church who are children of alcoholics. Chances are you are not alone and you could encourage and help each other.

Remove yourself. Don't hang around to observe your parents drunk. Get away from alcoholic scenes by taking a walk, visiting a friend, going to see a movie.

Carry a quarter. Always have a quarter on you so that you can leave the house, or wherever you are, and call a support person when things get too rough.

Safety first. If there is physical abuse or incest, consider your rights to live in a place free of violence. Turn to your local social services, your school, or your church for help.

Separate emotionally. Think about a life that is your own and, when ready, take the steps necessary to move out.

Intervene with parents. After learning as much as you can about alcoholism, you may try to work with the nondrinking parent in understanding the nature of the illness. But don't expect overnight changes. Keep your expectations realistic and don't try to be the family rescuer. Pray and leave the final results to God.

Take pride. Support yourself for having survived in an unhealthy environment and for having the courage to look at the situation for what it is. Build on the strengths you've acquired.

When a Friend Is a Victim

Claudette K. McShane also offers these tips for those dating a child of an alcoholic. However, her ideas can be applied to any friendship or relationship with someone who is a child of an alcoholic.

Be aware of the special characteristics of children of alcoholics. Read as much as you can about the topic so you can detect the most common problem areas.

Don't sanction or give permission for your friend's weaknesses. Instead, acknowledge the problem and let your friend develop an awareness that this is an issue which needs to be improved. Remember, permission can be given through silence, so remaining silent feeds the problem.

Don't make excuses for your friend's problems. It's easy to look the other way because of all the pain your friend has been through. But if you want this relationship to work, there's no excuse for destructive behaviors.

Be assertive when addressing problems related to growing up in an alcoholic household. Your friend may try to withdraw (a common trait) so don't play into it. Instead, state what you see, what you feel, and what you want.

Beware of alcoholic tendencies both in your friend and in yourself. A child of an alcoholic has a great chance of becoming addicted and, by being involved in a relationship with a child of an alcoholic, so do you. Get help if alcohol becomes a problem for either or both of you.

Seek support as a friend of a child of an alcoholic. Support groups are forming to aid individuals like you in your relationships with children of alcoholics. This can help you to know that you are not alone, and that the types of issues you're finding in your relationship are not unique.

If you are both children of alcoholics, find help through support groups or therapy. Your issues are compounded and your struggle toward closeness hampered by both of your backgrounds. A good therapist can aid in the growth of a healthy relationship.

Seek positive role models for your friend. Get your friend involved in a church where he or she can meet mature Christian adults.

Leave the relationship if it becomes too harmful to your physical or mental well-being.

Celebrate the strides you make in your growth as individuals and as a couple.

S I X

THE TEENAGE ABUSER AND THE FAMILY

AN INTERVIEW WITH MOTHER AND DAUGHTER

There are many aspects of drug and alcohol abuse that cannot be covered in the short quotes and stories offered in the preceding chapters. To really understand the dynamics of abuse, you must see real people.

It is impossible to convey the tension I felt during the following interview. Though I was a stranger to Anita Sanchez[1] and her mother until the interview, they revealed some of the deepest, most personal areas of their lives to me. Just reading the interview cannot show you the mother's shrugging shoulders, her tired, lifeless eyes, her worn features. It cannot show the way both mother and daughter shifted uncomfortably in their chairs. Nor can it show how I was affected for many days after the interview by mental fatigue and mild depression. There is no way a written interview can fully express these things.

Yet, this interview *can* explore factors in-depth that have only been hinted at throughout this book. Because all of these factors appear in the Sanchez family, and because I believe they are typical of homes where abuse is present, they are described briefly before the interview. Anyone who would consider being a problem solver, anyone who would consider showing compassion and understanding to those hurting from sub-

---

[1]Not her real name.

stance abuse, should examine these things carefully.

Denial. Not long ago, I watched a TV mini-drama about a high school student who died from smoking crack. Afterward, I talked with a friend who had also watched the program. She told me she thought the show was far from convincing. The denial expressed by the father, she said, was completely unbelievable; even after an autopsy proved the presence of cocaine in the son's body, the father still refused to believe his son had died from drug use. A few months back, I would have expressed the same incredulous feelings about the father's reaction.

Yet my recent research (and the research of many before me) gives strong evidence that the tendency toward such denial is tremendously strong, albeit irrational, in the parents of active and struggling abusers. One struggling abuser wrote me to say, "I was on pot for three years. I started drinking about six months after I started smoking pot. I'd come home totally stoned, wasted, or both. My parents didn't even notice— not even my father, who was a doctor in Vietnam where he worked with abusers all the time."

After my interview with Mrs. Sanchez and Anita, I came to believe in the power of denial. In outlining her long-term abuse, Anita offered example after example where her mother seemed to lack the ability to see what was happening around her. This was brought out even more powerfully when, in the interview, Anita revealed details about her abuse that were new to her mother. All this is not to say that Mrs. Sanchez is an uncaring mother. She seemed concerned about her children and especially about Anita's long-term pattern of abuse. In fact, Mrs. Sanchez currently teaches in an alternative school for "problem students," which includes students with drug and alcohol problems. Yet she appeared unable to "see" the devastation that had been taking place around her for several years.

Confusion over whether substance abuse is the root or the symptom of problem. In the first chapter we explored the question, "Why do users use?" Low self-esteem and a poor self-image were cited as reasons, though it is true that some kids use because of curiosity and others "just to have fun." But for many, even those reasons may be mere excuses and indications of deeper problems—as was the case for the struggling abusers who talked to me.

In Anita's case, abuse compounded her loneliness and feelings of a low self-worth. These feelings were increased by a rape (and its resulting abortion) that happened after she completed a "successful" eight-month treatment program. To deal with the abuse, yet not deal with the deep inner emotions and needs of the abuser, is not effective therapy.

Misunderstanding and misuse of alcohol. For some, alcohol brings terrible addiction. For others, it remains a social drink. For some it becomes a devastating killer through accidents, liver disease, and violence. For others, it's merely a harmless pastime. Alcohol fluctuates between two extremes: killer drug, harmless beverage. This creates a terribly confusing ambiguity that, I believe, continues to cause misunderstanding and misuse for many people.

Including Anita.

Even though she had been placed in the alcohol unit of a local hospital, even though she had drunk daily for an extended period of time, even though she experienced the "shakes" from alcohol withdrawal, even though she attends AA meetings, she still can't come to see herself as an alcoholic. She feels she can drink socially—something experts say is impossible for true alcoholics. At the end of the interview, Anita warned abusers that they will fall several times even after rehabilitation. In her own case, if her alcohol consumption continues, her words may indeed reflect a tragic truth.

Other factors. For Mrs. Sanchez, Anita's abuse was only part of the problem. It seemed that the system, time and again, worked against her and her daughter. After finally getting her daughter admitted into a treatment center, taking the long drive to the center, and waiting over three hours to receive attention from the center's staff, Mrs. Sanchez discovered that her daughter could not receive treatment. It seemed that her insurance was not adequate to pay the thousands of dollars the treatment would cost. Then the government said she simply made too much money to qualify for aid. Yet Mrs. Sanchez told me she could not possibly afford to pay for the treatment. For weeks Anita hung in limbo while parent and system haggled over paperwork. Admittance finally came after more abuse, suicide attempts, and prolonged family pain.

But the problems didn't end. There were long, hard drives on wintry days to visit Anita. And, because Mrs. Sanchez missed many days of work, she experienced continual tension with her employers. On one trip to see Anita, her sister and brother-in-law were involved in an accident that totalled their car. Also, there were arguments with Anita's grandparents over whether or not Mrs. Sanchez really needed to spend money on Anita's rehabilitation.

There were hassles with Anita's school, insensitivities on the part of some drug counselors, times of impatience and frustration on the part of all, and overall confusion and disagreement over how exactly to treat Anita. Worse of all, there was no guarantee that Anita would be cured after treatment.

Factors such as these often are missed when abuse is discussed. But we must realize that drug abuse does not happen in isolation. It invariably breeds more and more problems.

The lonely family. A psychologist friend recently told me that drug abuse often is just a symptom of a "social problem." That is, a total family—a dysfunctional family—often creates a situation where abuse can thrive. My friend stressed that the drug problem would not be solved until the entire family came to grips with the problems that may have created the abuse. Yet, Mrs. Sanchez is dealing with her daughter's abuse alone. Though she was advised to be involved in counseling with her daughter, she did not choose to do so. Though there are plenty of support groups for people in her situation, Mrs. Sanchez appeared unaware of them. She expressed the belief that other parents are generally unwilling to discuss their children's abuse.

Finally, I believe many parents remain trapped in some form of denial even after they "admit" to their child's problem. This denial is a trap that will make recovery—total recovery of the entire family—impossible. I hope this interview will alert many family members to the need for personal counseling and support. For it is in doing this that nonabusing parents and siblings can become more effective problem solvers in their own homes.

THE SANCHEZ HOUSEHOLD

Just before Anita started junior high, her mother moved the family from Mexico to Flint, Michigan, where they moved in with Mrs. Sanchez' parents. Prior to coming to the U.S., Mrs. Sanchez, a single parent, was a schoolteacher. Because her teaching credentials were invalid in Michigan, she was forced to work nights in a factory. So she enrolled in a local college to obtain a valid teaching license. After living a short time with her parents, Mrs. Sanchez and Anita's older brother, Louis, moved into a small apartment. However, Mrs. Sanchez thought Anita, who was in junior high, was too young to be alone while she worked the night shift and attended afternoon classes. So Anita's grandparents agreed to keep their granddaughter in their home. This living arrangement became a source of great tension for all concerned.

In time, Mrs. Sanchez bought a home and Anita came to live with her mother, her older brother, Louis, and her older sister, Marie, and brother-in-law, Mark, who had moved up from Mexico with them.

Anita, tell about your life right now.
Anita: I'm not living at home anymore. I just had to get away from my old life. Right now I'm living with a Christian family in Ann Arbor. I go to AA meetings once a week or every other week. Sometimes three times a week. So I do have some kind of treatment and I do see a therapist in Ann Arbor. I used to see the therapist once a week. Now I see her whenever it's necessary, if I feel I need to talk to her. So it's like once every three weeks.

What were you abusing?
Anita: It was alcohol and drugs. I would say about evenly between alcohol and drugs. But I started with speed in junior high.

How old were you then?
Anita: I was fourteen. I was in eighth grade. I don't even know why I took it. I was really scared when I first did it, 'cause I did not know the effects or what was going to happen. Like, was I going to see things or what? And all it did to me was tingle my head. I didn't really enjoy it. But it didn't scare me. I don't know if it was peer pressure that made me use. In a way I feel it was and in a way I feel it wasn't, 'cause it was my decision. I had asked for it. Actually, I had been offered it and said no, but later I came back and said, "Why not?" I think it was mostly that I wanted to try it and see what it was like. I wasn't really pressured by the kids until high school. That's when I started smoking pot.

Mrs. Sanchez, when your daughter was in junior high were you aware that she had tried drugs?
Mrs. Sanchez: No. Mothers are the last to know. No, I wasn't aware of it, I didn't even suspect.

Anita, how much were you using in junior high?
Anita: It was probably twice that I did speed. . . . Well, more than twice, but it was a few months between each time I took it.

How did you feel about doing speed and then coming home to your mother? Did you feel you had to hide your drug use?
Anita: At first.

Did you feel guilty?
Anita: Yeah, I felt guilty. I felt that there was something there I couldn't share with my mother. I guess it would have been possible to tell her, but it would have really been hard. So that kept me from saying, "Mom, I tried drugs." And it was hard because she wasn't home a lot.

Mrs. Sanchez, why weren't you home?
Mrs. Sanchez: You need to understand the background. We moved to the States in the summer of 1980 with a tennis racket, a hair curler, and a radio—that's all we had. Since my mom and dad live in the States, we started out living with them. We lived with them for about two or three months and then I got a job. But it was second shift. It was in a factory at eleven dollars an hour. It paid well so I was able to move and find an apartment for me, her older brother, Louis, who is in the service in Germany now, and my daughter Marie and her husband, Mark. It was a lovely apartment. But Anita had to stay with my mom because I had to work from three to eleven.

I thought she was too young to be in the house by herself. With my schedule, I would see her fifteen minutes a day, that was it. And I just didn't think a thirteen-year-old should be by herself after school. I mean, that's pretty hard to do. I thought it was better that she stay with my mother. At least she was around people. It was really hard for me to do this to her. And I think maybe at the time she didn't know how hard that was for me.

Anita, what were you thinking at the time?
Anita: When my mom told me that she had found an apartment, I was really excited. *Oh, we get to move,* I thought. *We get to have our own little place.* And then my mom says, "You have to stay here with Grandma, 'cause I'll be working second shift." At that time, I was feeling rejected and neglected.

Mrs. Sanchez: And then to top it all off, I had to work every Saturday. So I could only spend Sunday with Anita. So it was really hard.

Anita: It was really hard for me. I had problems with my grandparents, 'cause of my anger and stuff that I had inside.

Why were you angry?
Anita: It was because of Mom—I mean, I couldn't be with my mom. Because of the job. It wasn't that I didn't like my grandparents. I love my grandparents. But their values are, you know, pretty strict. Not real, real strict. But they know how to discipline. And that was hard for me;

when I lived in Mexico I was used to always having something to do. I had friends down the street. They would come over and we would go to the park. I was always doing something. But I came here to the States and didn't have any friends and I was stuck with my grandparents all the time. That's what I resented.

You resented the strictness?
Anita: And not having friends. I was new at school. I felt really lonely. There was nobody around on my own level.

How was your English at that point?
Anita: I could speak English well. I did have an accent. A little bit. It was more noticeable then. But I was really nervous about going to school because I couldn't read English very well. So that didn't help with adjusting to the whole situation of living here.

Anita, let's move up to your high school years.
Anita: Starting high school was like starting all over again. In junior high I had finally made a lot of friends, and they were really nice friends. But they lived in a different district so they went to a different high school. I was one of the very few people in that junior high to go to the high school I ended up at. So that was hard because I had to start all over with all new friends. But even though I felt lonely, I tried my best to make things work my freshman year. I was doing real good in school.

What kind of grades were you getting?
Anita: Fair grades. I had maybe a couple of A's, a couple of B's, maybe a couple of C's.

Mrs. Sanchez: Beginning her freshman year, she had above average scores on the Michigan Achievement Test.

Anita: But by November of my ninth-grade year, that fall, I smoked my first joint. I think it had a lot to do with the fact that I had nothing to do, no friends to be with. I'd sit at my desk and keep pretty quiet. I wasn't a leader type, never able to say, "Hi! My name is Anita, who are you?"

Where did you get the joint?
Anita: I heard about kids smoking pot and stuff. I knew a little bit about it. Not a lot. I knew that it did something to you. I didn't know if it made you feel good or funny or what. All I knew was that a lot of kids said it was great fun.

Then one day I found a wallet on the floor. I opened it to see whose it was and I found a joint. I found out who the wallet belonged to and I took him his joint. "Yeah, I'm going to smoke it," I told him. I was kind of playing around, yet I was wanting to try it. So he said, "Well, keep it." So I kept it. And it probably took me three days to smoke it. To even light it up, 'cause I was scared—but I was sold. So I smoked it on my way to school a few days later. And that was really weird. It lasted like three or four hours. And that was my first time. My second time, it was probably a week after that, I got really sick to my stomach. And then after that I didn't want to get sick again; I didn't do it for like three months. But eventually I forgot about how sick it made me, and remembered how it felt and how much fun it was the first time I used it. So when I was offered it again, I said sure. After that I smoked regularly throughout my freshman year.

Were you still living with your grandparents at this time?
Anita: No, by that time I was living here, at this house with my mom.

Mrs. Sanchez, were you still on the same work schedule?
Mrs. Sanchez: Uh huh. I stayed on that schedule for five years and then I quit. I walked out. I wish I had done it sooner. But I couldn't have left earlier, really. Economically, I couldn't have. We started out with nothing. We didn't have a car or anything. I had to pay for my schooling. When we were a bit better off, I decided to get out. But it was still tough. I had to get other work, finish my degree, manage the housework, take care of the kids, and make car payments. I don't know where we would be today if I had walked out on that job earlier. I don't know if it would have kept her from the drug problems, you know?

What do you say, Anita, looking back on it?
Anita: If she had quit earlier? Probably not. I don't think it would have kept me from my drug problem. I was already into it too deep to really care what happened anymore, you know. If she hadn't taken the job in the first place, then I might not have had this problem because I could have lived with my mother. I would have had somebody to be with me instead of my grandparents.

When you did manage to have time with your mother, were you able to open up and talk?
Anita: We could talk. When we first came here, we talked a lot; we were open then. After she moved and I had to stay with my grandparents we could still talk a little bit, but I was really hurt so I kind of backed away.

Mrs. Sanchez: You know that was less than a year that you had to do that.

She stayed with your parents for less than one year?
Mrs. Sanchez: Yes. We came in July of '80 and I bought this house and we moved into it in May of '81. When I moved into this house, she had her own room. She moved right into this house when I did.

But Anita was left alone a lot because you were still working in the factory?
Mrs. Sanchez: Yes, Anita was having some problems getting along with my parents, so I thought it was just better for her to stay with me. But she wasn't alone in the house for a minute. I rented rooms to college students too. Partly for money and partly so some people would always be coming in and out of the house. I wanted other young people around so she wouldn't be completely alone. She thought it was to baby-sit for her, but it wasn't. It was so she wouldn't be alone.
Anita: I still think it was baby-sitting.
Mrs. Sanchez: That really wasn't the purpose of it. My idea was to have more traffic in the house.

With everybody around, didn't someone detect that you were getting into drugs and drinking?
Anita: Nobody seemed to know. Not even my brother and sister. That was my secret.

When did your habit start getting heavy?
Anita: The summer before my tenth-grade year was a really lonely time. I was home alone. It was just my mother and I, mostly. My brother Louis was hardly ever around; he was in college by then. He was busy. Marie and her husband Mark were never around. So it was very lonely. I was alone all the time. And then I was afraid, you know, like a kid afraid of being left alone. So right after ninth grade I decided, "What the heck?" I didn't care. Nobody would catch me. My mom had wine in the house. And I would sit here and have the TV and the stereo on at the same time. I would sit here and think, *I'm bored, I'm lonely. I don't have anybody to do anything with. I think I'll get drunk.* I would say that and I would grab my mom's wine and get drunk on it. And then I could talk to the wall and I wouldn't be lonely anymore 'cause I was stimulated, you know, I was drunk.

We had a dog and I talked to my dog all the time. But then I would get really frustrated 'cause he wouldn't talk back. And that was really hard, you know. It was like, talk to me. You know how when you drink and get drunk, it's a downer and you get real depressed. Sometimes you cry for no reason. I would talk to my dog and then I would cry 'cause he wouldn't talk back. "Come on Pokey, talk to me," I'd say. And he would just look at me as if to say, "What's your problem?" I was very frustrated.

I wasn't satisfied. I wasn't satisfied with taking the dog for a walk instead of getting drunk, 'cause I had a bigger need. Someone to talk to, someone to goof around with, to ride a bike with or something like that. And so I remember I'd just sit here and I'd think, *Well, I'm bored, I'll get drunk now. It's that time.* And I remember for a whole summer, almost every day, at least once a week, I was getting drunk. And my mom, I don't know how she didn't know.

Did you ever wonder where the wine was going?

Mrs. Sanchez: She always gave me some good stories, some good reason why it was gone.

Anita: And sometimes my mom did ask, "Who's drinking my wine?" And I'd tell her, "I did. I had a glass." But I didn't. I had more than a glass. But I'd make it all sound so casual, like who could possibly care if I just had a little drink.

Mrs. Sanchez: I'd believe everything. I remember the time you said you just happened to lose a whole bottle of Louis' whiskey. And we believed you.

Anita: But it wasn't me that drank it. It still wasn't me, Mama.

Mrs. Sanchez: It still wasn't? We found the bottle in the attic, didn't we?

Anita: I did hide bottles up there.

You hid bottles in the attic?

Anita: I hid drugs up there too. Last time I was here, I was up in the attic going through my stuff, and I found a bag of marijuana seeds.

Mrs. Sanchez: Still?

Anita: Yeah, but I just tossed them. They wouldn't be any good anyway.

Mrs. Sanchez: There really was a suspicion in the back of my mind that something was going on. But I'd confront her with it and she'd always be ready with an answer. I'd believe her. Like the marijuana seeds I found in her bedroom. I can't remember how she said she had gotten them, but it was such a good story.

Anita: They're the ones you found under my mattress, right? I told her that they were left over from the first time I tried marijuana, but that was it. I said I wasn't doing it anymore and I forgot that they were even there.

Mrs. Sanchez: And I believed it.

Anita: But I was probably high at the time I told her that, too.

Mrs. Sanchez: And then there were those—what did you call those things with the feathers on them?

Anita: Roach clips.

Mrs. Sanchez: There were a couple of those hanging in her bedroom and I just thought they were some strange decorations. I didn't know what they were.

Let's get back to the summer before tenth grade. You were drinking quite a bit then?

Anita: Yeah. And when fall came I decided I was going to straighten up 'cause, you know, at the end of ninth grade my grades were pretty low. I hadn't failed any classes, but I was close to failing. So, I decided in tenth grade I was going to get my act together. I even took German, joined softball. So I was doing other things than just going to school.

Had you cut down on drinking because of these activities?

Anita: Yeah, I wasn't smoking marijuana either. I wasn't doing speed, because I wanted to get my act together—to get straight and do good in school. And for my first few weeks or whatever I was doing real well. I'd turn my homework in on time and I even did extra credit stuff. But then I got sick. I had strep throat. I missed two weeks of school and I got really behind. And then after that I got depressed. I just felt like I'd never be able to catch up.

So when I got back in school I started skipping classes and getting back into drugs to fill up my time. It was at that time that I started doing LSD. Toward the end of tenth grade, I started doing cocaine. So I was doing a lot. And I was drinking on top of everything. After a while, I was just going to school for the drugs. That's where I could get them. I hardly ever had to pay for them—people would just give them to me. I did have to pay a couple of times for the acid, LSD. But not usually—like the cocaine, I had a friend who was pretty wealthy and every time he got it he said, "Hey, I got some coke." I wasn't selling my body or selling things or anything to get drugs. That's one thing that made it real hard 'cause it was so easy. It was easy to say yes because I didn't have to spend any money.

So you were smoking and drinking a lot?

Anita: I was, yeah. I'd leave the house and I'd smoke a joint on the way to school. I'd smoke a joint in school. I'd smoke on the way home or drink or whatever. Sometimes I'd drink on the way to school. At the bus stop, a lot of kids drink.

What about the teachers? Didn't they know?

Anita: Well, a lot of them didn't know. In tenth grade I had gym class first hour. A friend of mine and I would show up early at the locker room so we could drink a couple of beers and smoke a joint. No one seemed to know. My teachers didn't know until one day when I was pretty drunk and high right before gym class. I walked out on the gym floor and they were doing jumping jacks. I just couldn't do it right. I thought I was doing them right, but I guess I wasn't. And my teacher called me up because she thought I was goofing off.

I was holding my breath so she couldn't smell me, but when she told me to run a lap, I said, "What? A lap?" And then she smelled that I had been drinking. I don't know if she could tell I was high. She could tell that something was wrong. So she made me stay with her all day and I had to miss my classes. I had to be with her in her classes. And by the end of the day I was sobered up and she told me, "I'm going to let you off this time, but next time I'm sending you to the office."

Well, according to the gym teacher, there was a "next time" and I got sent to the office. But that time I wasn't drunk or high. I was tired and I was probably hung over or something. I did look in sad shape. My eyes were red, baggy, and I was walking with my head down. They called my mom and when my mom came to pick me up she said, "Yeah, you look drunk, you look high." But I wasn't. I hadn't done anything that day. And it made me mad.

Mrs. Sanchez, how did you handle this?

Mrs. Sanchez: When I got this phone call, I came down pretty hard. The whole house went dry. No seltzer, no cooking sherry, not even rubbing alcohol—nothing. Then I asked the friends of the older children, "Please don't bring any alcohol into the house." And they didn't.

Anita, how did you react to these changes?

Anita: I was really, really mad, because this time I wasn't doing anything. And it all just made me more depressed.

Talk about that depression.

Anita: I didn't care about myself. My hair was getting real messy. It was hanging over my eyes. I'd wear just jeans and a T-shirt. I didn't feel good about myself. I didn't wash my face. I didn't wear makeup. I just looked really, really depressed 'cause I felt depressed. I would walk down the hall and my head was down low. It was getting lower as the time went by. I remember walking down the hall in high school and always looking at the floor—and half the time I didn't even realize it. The other half I was too ashamed to look up. I didn't want people to see how I was looking.

I always wanted better than this. I always wanted to be friends with the intellectuals—with those who like to study, or go to the museum, or just to have fun and go roller-skating and stuff like that. I wanted to be friends with those who dressed well. Those were the kinds of people I wanted to be with. I always wanted to act, to be in the drama club. But I couldn't 'cause my self-esteem was really low.

You were in a catch-22, weren't you? You wanted better but couldn't get it because you set your standards too low.
Anita: I started drinking and doing drugs to get some attention from others. My drinking wasn't to get drunk, even though I did get drunk. It was more for the attention. I wanted somebody to show they cared. But then my brothers and sisters started showing more like anger, like, "Bad Girl Anita, the troublemaker."

I felt like they had always left me out and I didn't care about their feelings. See, they are so much older than I am. They could leave any time they wanted. They would go to movies and I could never get in because they always chose R-rated movies. My feeling was they were going to go see an R-rated movie on purpose so I couldn't go. Now I look back and that was not true. It was just that the movie they happened to want to see was rated R and I couldn't get in. So I felt really rejected by my brothers and sisters.

I was just feeling very sorry for myself. I would have a lot of pity parties. A lot of them. There was this staff member from a Christian club at school who I think played into my attention-seeking a lot. She seemed to really care, and it went to my head. So I just started seeking her attention a lot.

You mean you would keep using drugs and drinking to get more of her attention?
Anita: Yeah. A lot of it was attention-seeking to fill the loneliness. She would say to me, "Why are you doing this?" But then I'd do more drugs and drink more alcohol, 'cause it would just make her more concerned, more interested in me. First I was drinking to fulfill my loneliness, then I was drinking to get drunk, and then I was drinking and doing drugs for

the attention. Then when I got the attention I wanted more. It wasn't enough. It never was enough. If I got a little more today, I thought maybe I could get even more tomorrow. And then there were days when I didn't get any at all. And those were my real bad days.

Of course, after a while it wasn't so much attention-seeking as dependence on the substance. I wasn't addicted to pot. Pot was something I liked to do. I had a hard time with alcohol after a while 'cause if I didn't drink, I would get the shakes. And I'd get sweaty. It was hard to not drink 'cause I would get really nervous. It wasn't a pleasurable feeling. It was like something is missing.

And that's the same with the cocaine and the LSD. I tried acid once and then I didn't do it for a long time. Then I did it again. And then I was doing it again, and again, and again. I was doing like one or two dots a day. And then I got addicted to the acid. I'd take one and as soon as I'd start coming down from it, which is like nine hours later, I would take another one 'cause I didn't want to come down. I'd eat the dots of acid like candy.

How could you function in the classroom?
Anita: When I was doing LSD I started skipping a lot of classes. I hid in bathrooms, or my friends and I would just leave the school grounds. There was a park right across the street from the high school. I would go there and swing or walk around. When I was in the classroom, I always made sure I sat way in the back in the corner. I could be in my own little world.

Mrs. Sanchez: What about on the weekends?

Anita: I used mostly on the weekends when you weren't around. Sometimes Mom would go to Chicago and visit friends. Most of the times I had to go with her. But there were times when somebody was going to be here and it was OK for me to stay home. And those were the times when I would go up in the cemetery and get high or do acid. Everybody else was too busy to notice anyway. It wasn't every weekend; it was mostly during the week.

Mrs. Sanchez: There weren't many weekends that I wasn't home, though. When we first moved here I never, never did anything on the weekends that she couldn't do with me. But when I'd go to Chicago she'd always go with me and we'd have a ball together.

Anita, was that your perception at the time?
Anita: Well, when I went with my mom to do things we always had a good time.

Mrs. Sanchez: One time we took the bus and trains and went to all those Chicago museums. We just had a really good time together. I had friends that had a house on Lake Michigan. I'd spend time with them and she was always with me. I never, never went without trying to take my daughter because I didn't want to leave her alone. Well, it got to the point where she would say, "No, I don't want to go." I don't think she realizes to this day all the things that I turned down because I didn't want to leave her alone. I knew that something wasn't right. But I didn't know what it was. And I really didn't want to leave her alone.

It got so I didn't want to go anyplace, 'cause she didn't want to go anyplace. Probably by then she was so high on whatever.

Anita: When I got home from school my mom would get really sick of me because all I'd do was lie on the couch. And my mom would say, "Well hey, I've got fifteen minutes before I go to work. Don't you want to eat?" She'd usually have dinner waiting.

Mrs. Sanchez: Yeah, we'd have fifteen minutes to eat and I'd have the dinner table all set. That was our fifteen minutes a day together.

Anita: It got to the point where I didn't even want dinner. I remember one day my mom expressed her feelings about that and said, "I'm getting sick of you coming home and lying on the couch and never eating with me!"

Mrs. Sanchez: It was really frustrating for me, because it was the only time together we had in the day. It got to the point where I'd eat alone and her plate would sit there and get cold.

Anita: I'd just lie on the couch or go to my room.

Mrs. Sanchez: On weekends when we could do something together, she never wanted to do it. I finally did things by myself. But I turned down more things. She remembers the times I went, but I'm sure she doesn't know about the times I didn't go because I never really complained to her about it. I still don't feel like I gave anything up.

People talk a lot about how the child or the young adult feels in a situation like this, but attention is rarely given to the parent. How did you feel during all of these problems?
Mrs. Sanchez: I felt sad. I just felt sad. And I felt stupid because she had been doing it for so long and I hadn't known. See, there's kind of a feeling in the back of my mind that my daughter wouldn't do that.

Let's talk about that feeling. You must know that it is very typical for a parent to deny her child's abuse or not to even realize it's going on. You said the mother is the last to know. That's a typical reaction.

Mrs. Sanchez: I don't really know that much about it. I mean, I don't know any other parents that have gone through this. Oh, I do know other parents who have gone through this, but they never talk about it.

You never got involved in a support group?
Mrs. Sanchez: No, I couldn't because of my job and my school. There was just no time. Dr. Schmidt, a counselor friend at the college I attended, insisted that I go to one. But it just didn't work with my schedule. It also didn't seem like it was something people talked about.

One particular situation really sticks in my mind. Anita had been taking piano lessons right before going in for treatment. I finally had to call the piano teacher to say, "Sorry, she won't be needing piano lessons anymore." And I can't lie, and this is really hard for me, but I went ahead and said, "She's going to a drug rehabilitation program." And the piano teacher said, "Oh, I'm so sorry to hear that. We had a problem like that with one of our daughters." And that was all I heard about this person's situation. Each time I told someone about Anita's problem, because I never lied about it, others would tell me of similar problems.

It helped others open up, maybe?
Mrs. Sanchez: They didn't really. They never told me what they went through. But just by them mentioning a problem, I found out how many other people have gone through this with their children. I mean, these are well-educated people. And they all did get help for their kids. But the fact that they too had a problem like this was surprising to me.

What was it like that first time you admitted that your daughter had a problem?
Mrs. Sanchez: I didn't admit it. I didn't admit it for a long time. I still can't believe it. I got help for my daughter without believing she had trouble.

What do you mean?
Mrs. Sanchez: She thought she had the problem. And if she thought she had a problem, I'd help her.

Anita: And eventually my teachers thought something needed to be done.

Mrs. Sanchez: I still have trouble believing it.

Why do you think you continue to deny that there was a problem?
Mrs. Sanchez: I couldn't believe it. I didn't know any alcoholics, any people with drug problems. I just couldn't believe it. I mean even after

the school called me that first time about the gym class incident, I still couldn't believe it. I guess the first time I really said to myself, "Maybe we do have a problem here," was when she had gone to school with red wine in a transparent plastic Coke bottle. Now, that tells you something.

You mean you thought red wine could pass for Coke?
Anita: It was white wine. I thought I had a 7-Up bottle. If I had had a 7-Up bottle, I don't think I would have gotten caught.

It sounds like you were taking a lot of risks.
Anita: I drank it right in the parking lot.

Mrs. Sanchez: Some teachers caught her in a car in the school parking lot. They called my mother, because I was at work at the time. They said they were sending Anita home right away on the city bus. So my mother called me and I called the school right back. I said, "Do not send my daughter home on the city bus. I'm coming to pick her up. Do not put her on that city bus." When I got there, they said she had already left. I have never been so angry in all my life. I said, "I'm trying to monitor my daughter's every move. I do not want her to take the city bus." It got me so upset. It just didn't seem right. They gave her the money to put her on the city bus. And I said, "You think she's going home? She's not going to come home knowing what's waiting for her at the house with me knowing that she's been caught with wine at school."

Did you come home?
Anita: Yeah, uh huh. At first I wasn't going to come home. I thought if I could just leave right now, just run away . . . but then I thought I should face it. I'd be better off.

Mrs. Sanchez: And that was probably the turning point for me. And my kids started helping out a lot. In fact, Marie, my oldest daughter, and her husband, Mark, went through hell trying to help Anita. Mark would literally grab her and not let her leave the house. Physically grab her and make her stay home when I was at work. Louis, the son that's in Germany, went to get her one time and she was drunk and couldn't walk home. All the kids were really angry at her for doing this and tried to keep her from doing it. Probably Marie suffered the most because Marie cared so much. Marie just went through a whole lot trying to help her.

Anita: Marie has a big heart. The more my brother and sister and her husband found out about the problem, the more they showed they cared. But I resented them all a lot. I felt like they were trying to control me. I would get mad.

Mrs. Sanchez, you believed she was crying for help. But what kind of help? Did you believe she had an alcohol problem?
Mrs. Sanchez: I thought of depression; I thought of teenage suicide—there's a lot of that happening. I became very worried about that. After she was caught with the wine, I monitored her every minute I could. I'd drive her down to the school bus stop. There were times when she would get very angry and say, "Mom, you think I'm a kindergartner by taking me down to the bus stop."

When did you begin to seek help for chemical and alcohol dependence?
Mrs. Sanchez: A friend of mine was one of the bilingual teachers at Anita's school and a former counselor at a drug program in Minnesota. I knew her from the college I was attending. She talked to me about what had happened and she said right off the top of her head, "I'd say your daughter has some kind of substance abuse problem." And I said, "You're the counselor, you have more experience than I do." And so she started looking for a rehabilitation program for us. One thing she discovered, and couldn't believe, was that in the local area there were no places for teenagers to go. There was zero at that time. It was incredible that it was so hard to find treatment in this part of the state.

We decided to try the next city over. My friend found a brand new center in Lansing about thirty miles from here. So she looked into it and talked with Anita. We made a couple of trips over there. And my friend went with us each time because she wanted to find out more about it. So, finally, everything was all set. They evaluated Anita, they accepted her—everything was all set. She packed up. Said good-bye. We let the people at school know she wouldn't be there for six weeks.

Anita, how did you feel at this point? Were you ready to get some help? Did you want to change or did you feel you were being forced into something?
Anita: I was told by my mom's friend that as a minor I could be forced; I could become a ward of the court. So I decided, why go to all that trouble of fighting if I have to go anyway?

Did you feel you had a drinking and drug problem?
Anita: Not physically, but emotionally. And I felt I had brought it on myself.

Did you feel you needed help?
Anita: I knew I needed help. But the kind of help I really wanted was attention and friends. I didn't want to be in the house alone. I felt that if I

could get some friends and get some attention and not be lonely, then it would go away by itself. But I did make the decision to go into rehabilitation, and then it took me a while to feel comfortable with that decision. When I did feel comfortable with my decision, I wanted to get straight. And I had a lot of support from a lot of people. Many said they'd write me.

Friends from school?
Anita: Not friends from school. Some teachers, but not friends. Friends would say, "So you're going to rehab, see ya later." But family members and friends who live in this neighborhood showed they cared.

By "see you later," you mean they abandoned you?
Anita: Yeah. Like, "You're not my friend." I don't know if that's what they meant, but that's how I took it. But I really don't know what they meant by that. But I did have a lot of support from a lot of people.

Mrs. Sanchez, what happened next in getting Anita help?
Mrs. Sanchez: When we arrived at the treatment center we had to sit for three hours, because the director was in a meeting. Then they came down, after we had waited three hours, and said, "Sorry, your daughter can't come here. Your insurance won't pay for it." So after saying goodbye to everybody, after Anita had made that big decision to get treatment, she couldn't get in. It was frustrating. I was angry. I was angry to think that my daughter had finally agreed to do this and she couldn't get help.

Where did you go from there?
Mrs. Sanchez: I had a big fight with the insurance company, writing letters to my state representative complaining that my insurance would not take care of it. I went through all of that. Then I tried—Anita doesn't even know this—the county health program. Then another treatment center. I couldn't get her into any of these places.

Why not?
Mrs. Sanchez: Money. They're expensive. I mean *expensive*. The first center, the one my friend found for us, costs twelve thousand dollars for six weeks. And, of course, no treatment is guaranteed, so you could pay that more than once and still not get anywhere. Where do you come up with that kind of money when you haven't been in the States that long? When you have absolutely no assets? Where do you come up with that money? You don't. You can't. I couldn't have even borrowed it. No collateral. I could have sold the house, but I couldn't because it was under

contract. If I had sold the car, how could I earn more money? There was no way I was going to come up with that money. I thought it wasn't fair that my insurance wouldn't take care of it. And then there was the county health program. According to the system, I just earned too much money to get any aid or special help from the state. But I did not earn enough, not nearly enough to pay for any kind of treatment. I wonder how many people are out there like myself.

Because it was a little cheaper than a live-in center, we tried private counseling for a while. The cost was supposed to be based on your income, but it still cost me between $50 and $65 an hour. And they always wanted the sessions to go for like twice a week for an hour each time. So that ran me between $100 and $140 a week. And since Marie and her husband Mark were living with me at the time, I had five people to feed.

I called so many places, so many people. Some people would be sympathetic toward us. Other people would be like, "Too bad, tough luck." I was using all of my free time trying to find help for my daughter. We tried [a nationally known support group], which was free. In this program, a parent is supposed to go with her child. I went to the first session, but after that I asked Marie to go for me since I couldn't afford to miss any more work. I had already missed a lot of work because of her problem and my bosses were getting very upset with my absentee record.

Tell me a bit more about the support group.
Mrs. Sanchez: Anita hated it. I guess Marie and Anita had a run-in every week when they were supposed to go. Marie would come home crying. It was putting Marie through hell. And it really wasn't Marie's problem. Why should she have to do this?

Marie was acting as a parent at this point?
Anita: Right. It worked kind of like this. Teens would be in one group and the parents or guardians would be in a different group. They would ask each group real personal questions.
   Mrs. Sanchez: It was just breaking Marie up. She'd come home and she'd cry a lot. And she'd cry because of what Anita was doing. She'd be angry at Anita. Angry at her one minute and the next minute just feeling sorry that we couldn't help her. And at the support group they finally told Marie, "If your mother really wanted to come, she'd be here." Well, I mean, how could they tell my daughter that? So I told Marie, "That's it, Marie. Don't go anymore." Why did she have to go through that? She was doing it as a favor to me.

Then I finally read a little blurb in the student newspaper at the college I was attending. It was about Dr. Schmidt who had this counseling service for substance abusers among the college students. That's when I finally called Dr. Schmidt.

When Dr. Schmidt started counseling Anita, he felt her problem was so severe that he had her immediately admitted into an alcoholic unit of a local hospital. She was in there five days. By then I was really getting a lot of pressure from my parents. They had been against treatment all along. They kept telling me, "Oh, don't put her in the hospital. That's not necessary. She is not an alcoholic. She shouldn't be there. You shouldn't be spending your money on this." I mean, I was just under a lot of pressure.

Did you think your daughter was an alcoholic at this point?
Mrs. Sanchez: Nope.

Do you feel she's an alcoholic now?
Mrs. Sanchez: I thought it was more drugs than alcohol. Truthfully, I still don't know if she's an alcoholic. I do not offer my daughter a beer and I don't think I ever will. I will not have a glass of beer in front of her. In the past, there had always been something to drink in the house. But I don't think there's any alcohol in the house now. The drug part is what frightens me more than the alcohol. Yet the people at the hospital felt she had a definite problem. They know more about alcoholism than I do. So I've just kind of been taking the experts' word for it.

What about you, Anita, do you think you're an alcoholic?
Anita: I don't think I am now. I feel like I can be. If I started drinking heavy again, I could have a problem. I do have a beer once in a while. I like the refreshment of it. Before, I was drinking to get drunk for the attention. But now it's more for the refreshment. Or a social drink. I do like beer. I learned to like it. Now I can really enjoy the taste. I do know that I can become really dependent. So I go to AA meetings.

Mrs. Sanchez: Just a minute . . . this man has come to interview you about all your problems, and you tell him you're still doing it?
At this point in the interview there was an uncomfortable silence. I decided to move back to focusing on Anita's time in rehabilitation.

Anita, talk some more about your time with Dr. Schmidt.
Anita: When I started my evaluation time with Dr. Schmidt, before I got put in the alcohol wing, things got pretty tough. After a while it hurt to come down from cocaine. A couple times I would just bear the pain. A

lot of times I would just go to bed and try to sleep it away. But sometimes it was really hard. During this time I was sneaking some cocaine, which really didn't help. If I did some cocaine, it was hard to get some more because I was watched pretty closely. If I did manage to sneak say, two lines, and I'd come down, it was only a slight pain. It wasn't that bad. It was the type of pain I could bear. But if I'd snuck like four lines that day, it was more pain, so it was harder.

Mrs. Sanchez, were you aware at this time that along with the alcohol she was also doing cocaine?
Mrs. Sanchez: No.

You don't remember any symptoms of cocaine use, like nasal problems?
Anita: There was a lot of times when my nose was bloody, but I kept it from her.
Mrs. Sanchez: When she started meeting with Dr. Schmidt I still didn't know much about what was going on. Her meetings with him were confidential. But he did say to me, "Believe me, you have a problem." And there are a lot of things, I still don't understand. Like "lines" of cocaine. Today is the first I heard that expression. I thought you had used coke maybe two times in your life.

Anyway, she continued to see Dr. Schmidt the rest of that year and had to finish her tenth-grade year in the alternative education school—a school for students with special problems. When she entered the alternative ed school the next fall, her eleventh-grade year, the problems continued. She even ended up at the suicide unit at the local hospital.

You tried to commit suicide?
Anita: Yes. I was very, very depressed. I overdosed on LSD. I wasn't trying to die from the drug. But I thought if I took enough dots I might get crazy enough to jump in front of a car or something else. Or fly or something.

So you were self-destructive?
Anita: Yeah. I mixed it with alcohol. I was drinking a bottle on the way to school; I finished my bottle by the time I got to school and I grabbed some dots and took a whole handful. But they didn't have any effect on me. It didn't make me hallucinate. It didn't make me trip at first. By the very end of the day when I was supposed to hop on the bus, I missed it. I remember I was trying to be calm, but my anxiety level was going sky high 'cause I was waiting for that effect and it wouldn't come, and it

wouldn't come, and it wouldn't come. Finally it did, and the school officials called my mom and told them I'd missed the bus.

By the time she got there, I'd gone haywire. What happened was that I ran out into the street and was pulling my hair and screaming. The principal grabbed me and dragged me into a classroom. They had to remove all the desks and all the chairs, because I was throwing things. And he held me there and he said, "You've obviously taken something. What have you taken?" By then I was really out of it. I was just real spaced out. By then I felt like I was flying and then I was satisfied. I was satisfied then.

Mrs. Sanchez: When I finally got to the school one of the teachers was walking her in the hallway. We immediately put her in the car and I took her right to the hospital.

Anita: And they pumped my stomach. After that, I tried many times to commit suicide.

Mrs. Sanchez: Those suicide attempts frightened me so much. It just seemed to keep getting worse. And the bills kept mounting up. Along with seeing Dr. Schmidt, we were going to the hospital for more evaluations and she was also seeing a psychiatrist. I'm paying off these doctor's bills at five dollars a week for the rest of my life. The psychiatrist would evaluate her one way and Dr. Schmidt would give a different evaluation. So many different places to go to by then. Appointments and evaluations. I kept getting bills and bills and bills. But I never told her about the money.

Anita: I sensed that there was a lot of money involved, and that was a very big guilt trip for me. And that was one of the reasons I kept doing drugs even during counseling—to escape the guilt.

Mrs. Sanchez: For me the money problem was just made worse by all the pressure I received from my parents, who felt Anita's problem wasn't because of drugs or alcohol. But the ball really got rolling when she was evaluated as suicidal and sent to Woodhaven.

Where is Woodhaven?
Mrs. Sanchez: That's in Ann Arbor.

And that is where you ended up getting long-term treatment?
Anita: Yes.

When was that?
Anita: It was four weeks before Christmas in '84. At that time I went for a one-week evaluation. Then I had to go on a waiting list. I didn't actually enter the center for treatment until March 1, 1985.

And again, more waiting?
Mrs. Sanchez: Yeah. She ended up going into a hospital suicide ward until we could get her into Woodhaven. It could have cost us thousands of dollars for a six-week stay at Woodhaven and her total stay turned out to be for eight months. But it was finally worked out through social services and the insurance company, and we didn't have to pay. Yet it was still a lot of hassle. The hospital was four hours from here. I had to go up twice a week. Work, my schooling, and the winter really made the drive rough.
Anita: I had a big guilt trip over that too.

Why did you feel guilty?
Anita: I felt bad because of all the driving she had to do. By then I was also regretting all of my behavior. I was feeling really bad. One thing that got me real depressed was that my brother-in-law and my sister came up to visit and visiting hours only lasted one hour. So it was like eight hours on the road for a one-hour visit. And then on the way back they got in an accident and totalled their car. I felt so responsible, and then my suicidal thoughts started coming back. Because of my feelings I would even abuse myself. I got scars from cutting myself. I was self-destructive. I would burn myself with a curling iron. I would do a lot of things. And that was because I was angry with myself. I was taking it out on myself. And at that time I wasn't so much suicidal, as I was trying to punish myself. I felt so guilty. I felt responsible for my sister's accident. I felt responsible for my mom taking all the time off work, and all the money she could have earned while she was coming to see me.

What was it like being at Woodhaven?
Anita: At first, things didn't change much. I still wasn't totally off drugs during part of my treatment. I wasn't doing heavy drugs, but I was still smoking pot.

You could get drugs at Woodhaven?
Anita: Patients would smuggle it in. After so many weeks of being there, you could go home like every other weekend. So I had this friend there who would go home and come back with pot and I would smoke it with her. The whole time I was at Woodhaven, I never ever brought any drugs back from a weekend visit. It was her. And I'm not blaming her for my use. I'm the one who made the decision. It started out with one joint. Then it was two joints the next time. And it was bags, and bags, and bags. I don't know how she brought them in. We were getting high a lot. This probably went on for a month and a half.

The nurses that worked with me could tell that something was wrong because my eyes were bloodshot from smoking. And my mouth was really dry. And one particular nurse said, "Your eyes are red. Have you been crying? Are you depressed?" I said, "Sure." I'm not going to say I'm high. If I say that, they're going to lock me up in the QR, which is a room with nothing in there, so it protects you.

What does QR stand for?
Anita: Quiet Room. But I wouldn't admit to smoking. I would say, "Yeah, I'm depressed." Then we'd have to talk about it. So we'd talk about why I'm depressed. I wouldn't lie about my depression. So we talked about my past. But it was tricking them.

Then I did get caught because they started keeping closer tabs on my vital signs which would, of course, show that I was using some kind of substance. After I got caught, I realized I had blown my chance to go to college. See, the weekend I got caught I was coming home to interview for financial aid. And they caught me so they took my privilege away. They also added a couple of months to my stay.

It wasn't until probably halfway through my treatment at Woodhaven I decided this is it. I'm going to be real. I want to be happy. I've done many things to be happy, but they've all been negative things. I'm going to do positive things now.

So I was doing creative art. I did a cross-stitch picture for a nurse I was close to. I was doing a lot of things now. Everything that I made at Woodhaven, I gave away. I never kept anything for myself. It made me happy to do that. I was starting to look better. My nurse friend started saying things like, "Your skin looks so much better. You don't have bags under your eyes. You look alive." And I needed to hear that.

One thing that really helped me a lot during the treatment was the monthly evaluations. During those evaluations they would give me a lot of positive feedback, but also some constructive criticism. At times I would take it as, "You guys are blind. I'm trying so hard to do what's right, to do good in this program, and you guys are blind. You can't see that." But they weren't being negative. They were saying, "Yeah, you're doing good, but this is an area you have to work at." And it took a while for that to sink in.

What were some of those areas?
Anita: A lot of it was my motivation. I didn't have a whole lot of motivation because of the drugs I had been using. They made me tired all the time. Even though I wasn't doing drugs, it was really hard for me to start back up and get motivated. To this day, it's still hard. I didn't have any

initiative at all. I had to be told, "Do your assignment." I wouldn't do my class work—I was working on the twelfth-grade year of school there—and I would just be sitting there talking with someone or reading a book or something. And someone would come along and say, "Anita, do your assignment." My initiative was really bad.

So, I had to get motivated. I started riding my bike a lot—there was a bike at Woodhaven I could use. I would go for a lot of walks, trying to get my energy back up. I was eating healthier. Instead of eating candy bars, I'd eat an apple. I felt different physically. And that made me feel real good about myself. It wasn't till about halfway through the treatment at Woodhaven that I realized something important about the staff there. They weren't there for the money. They were there because they really cared. And they really showed it.

The people showed a lot of love?
Anita: They really showed it.
Mrs. Sanchez: It's a Christian treatment center. That was another thing. When I was trying to find treatment for my daughter, I wanted a Christian hospital. I wanted a positive, Christian environment.
Anita: We had chapel every Sunday. We could decide whether or not to go. I went most of the time.

What were some other tough times during treatment?
Anita: My friend that was bringing drugs in, they didn't want me to hang around with her so much. So they limited our time together. They would set what they called "a peer boundary." This is where we couldn't get any closer than ten feet to each other. And we couldn't sit with each other at dinner. We couldn't go into each other's rooms. So they limited my time with negative friends or peers. They had me spend time with positive peers. Even though I didn't like some of them, I had to bear with it.

They put me in a special program where I would have to spend two hours alone in my room. During that time I would have to write a paper on how I felt or whatever. And that was really hard for me because I thought, *Here I am, I'm going to be lonely again.* But even though it was hard, it was good therapy. Then I had a lot of one-on-one meetings with the staff, where we would try to talk things out. Those got pretty intense sometimes.

Sometimes I would hide from the staff. I did have my bad days. But it was a good program. The first month was really the worst. I was really down. I was really depressed, I felt like I had defeated myself, like I was cheating myself. I felt like I wasn't working to my capability. But I also felt like there must be more. I must have more potential. Other times were more upbeat, like doing something creative, like sewing some shorts or doing cross-stitch.

Anita, have you had any setbacks since you finished treatment?
Anita: Yeah. I finished my treatment and then I came back home. I felt real good and was ready to start over. I even got a job. And then I got depressed again 'cause this friend, someone that was supposedly a friend, raped me.

When I went into the treatment center, he was one person I thought really cared. He would write me letters and say, "You're going to do fine, I'll help you when you get out. I'll even go to AA meetings with you." He was a real neat friend. And then when I got out of Woodhaven and I was working at Montgomery Wards, I ran into him. It was really good to see him again. So I asked him over to our house after work. When he got here we were alone in the house together and he raped me. And so I fell back again.

I remember I probably smoked a couple of joints to get over that. I didn't know what to do. And I didn't want to tell my mom, because I figured she wouldn't understand. What I really needed was support and I didn't know if I could get that from Mom. So I told a girlfriend of mine and I told her I didn't know what to do. At that time, I didn't know if I was going to be pregnant.

So I did fall back. I did smoke some pot to deal with that, to cope. I got depressed again. So I went back to Woodhaven for six weeks to the adult unit because by then I was eighteen. I dealt with it. Not a lot. I would avoid the staff because I didn't want to talk about it. It was something really hard to talk about. I feel I wasn't there enough time to really deal with it.

After I got out, I decided to stay in Ann Arbor. I met a family there who were willing to keep me in their home without charging me rent.

You wanted to stay in Ann Arbor to keep away from the guy who raped you?
Anita: Yeah. Nothing against my family or anything, but I wanted to leave them here too. I met a real nice family in Ann Arbor and stayed there. And I never told my mom this, this is going to be the first time for her to hear this, but I had to get an abortion. I did get pregnant through the rape. I never told my mom I had an abortion. I just didn't want to live with that memory [of the rape] if I kept the child. I didn't want to live with that memory.

Mrs. Sanchez: And to think that Marie is out there picketing Planned Parenthood.

Anita: Marie knows.

Mrs. Sanchez: She knows?

Anita: Marie and I are really close. I could share with her. I didn't go into detail. But I told her all this. I came home one night and Marie was here with her baby and I had a hard time seeing her child and knowing I hadn't kept mine. By then I regretted having had the abortion, 'cause I do not believe in abortion. And I did not believe in premarital sex. So it was really hard—I felt like I had killed someone. I felt guilty. So I left everything behind and moved to Ann Arbor. I did go to a rape crisis center there and to abortion group therapy. But this is new to my mom, I haven't shared this with her. I don't know why I haven't shared.

So the abortion made me feel real guilty. I'd killed an innocent person. A baby, a child. So then I started smoking again. And it was only a couple of times that I got high and that's when I realized, *This is stupid. I'm just making matters worse.*

Anita, what kind of advice would you like to give to teenagers who are struggling with drug abuse?

Anita: For anybody who has a drug problem or an alcohol problem: Be prepared to fall back, because you're going to. Whether you like it or not, you're going to. Like, for instance, there's a death in the family; you're going to go hit the bottle. So be prepared for that. But you have to realize that if you fall back, don't keep going back. Learn from your mistakes.

In my life I've made a mistake and I've learned from it. I don't think, *Oh how stupid. That was dumb.* It's OK. I made a mistake. It's like learning to ride a bike. You ride for a while, then you fall. You don't dwell on it. You get up and you try again. And that's one thing that I really stress to people is to try and try and try again. The only time you're ever going to fail is when you don't try. In fact, my middle name became Anita "Try Again" Sanchez. I was nicknamed that because I would try and try again.

Do you feel you're making strides forward again?

Anita: Right now, a year since I had the abortion, I'm doing good in life.

What other advice would you give to teenagers who are struggling with drug abuse?

Anita: You have to find things to do with your spare time. You have to have something to take the place of the drugs. Sometimes I feel like drinking a beer or something. I've had a bad day and I admit, "Oh, today is one of those days I could get drunk and I could care less." But if I do that it's not going to help me at all. So I've got to think of something to take up that time that I would use to get drunk. I bought a bike. I'm biking a lot now. I bought a car. I can go places.

There's another thing I'd like to stress: Don't be afraid to take risks. Risks are how you grow. At Woodhaven I went through this wilderness camping program, and we had to walk on rope bridges thirty-five feet up in the air, and we had to climb steep walls with just a rope. I look back and I think, *I climbed a forty-five-foot wall! If I can climb a forty-five-foot wall, I can do anything. I can get a job. I can confide in someone that I have a problem.* Those are risky things for me. But if you don't take risks, you don't grow. I've grown a lot.

Also, learn that you can be happy. For me, helping people makes me happy. If I don't help people, I'm not happy. So, I get depressed again.

Mrs. Sanchez, what advice would you give to parents?

Mrs. Sanchez: Listen to your suspicions. If you suspect something, believe it is probably true.

Then another thing. I know that other people will face the financial situation I faced if they try to get help. Just keep trying and eventually you'll get help. The way we finally got around the system was to have her declared "independent" when she reached eighteen. That way I couldn't claim her on my taxes anymore and it became easier to get financial aid from social services.

You must also realize that your kids are responsible for their actions. At first I had guilt feelings, like it was all my fault. I just came to my own conclusion: I didn't make her take drugs.

And you can't stop loving them. I tried that once. The day she took the wine in the Coke bottle, I said, "That's it. I don't love you anymore. I don't care." I felt bad and that lasted thirty minutes. That was the end of that. It doesn't work. I know she accused me a lot of not loving her.

Anita: But I knew deep inside that she did love me.

Mrs. Sanchez: It hurts too much to see your daughter do such things to herself.

PART THREE

THE SEARCH FOR ANSWERS THAT WORK

SEVEN

WHAT TO DO?

When students were asked about solving the drug and alcohol problem, only about two-thirds offered possible solutions. The other third simply did not express an opinion or felt a solution can not be found. The largest percentage (17 percent) said "educate about what drugs do." The following areas received about equal (low) numbers of supporters: positive peer pressure (8 percent), voluntary programs (6 percent), group counseling (6 percent), less talk and more action (6 percent).

One out of ten guys view going to jail for drug use as a solution, while it received no support from girls in the survey sample. Another difference between male and female solutions was the response to "show that life is fun without drugs." Six percent of the females gave that solution thumbs up, while it received no male support. It is noteworthy that a greater number of females gave positive feelings about solutions than did males.

Another interesting finding was the low number of teenagers (2 percent) who offered "dealing with underlying problems" as a solution. I can't help but hope that those who read Anita's story in the previous chapter will see the necessity of getting beyond the superficials of drug use to the real struggles, feelings, and pain within.

Finally, such low percentages for all these "solutions" would seem to indicate that most students are not optimistic about solving the drug and alcohol problem.

CHART 5 **HOW TO SOLVE THE PROBLEM**

What would be the best way for a drug and alcohol program to really help people?

	MALE	FEMALE	TOTAL
Educate about What to Do	16%	19%	17%
Positive Peer Pressure	6%	12%	8%
Programs, Voluntary Only	4%	8%	6%
Group Counseling	4%	8%	6%
Less Talk/More Action	6%	3%	5%
Jail/Use Laws/Police	10%	0%	5%
Make Them Quit	9%	0%	5%
Be Loving/Caring	1%	5%	3%
Current Programs Are Fine	4%	2%	3%
There Is No Good Way	4%	2%	3%
Show That Life Is Fun Without Drugs	0%	6%	3%
Individual Counseling	1%	3%	2%
Test for Drugs	4%	0%	2%
Scare Tactics	3%	2%	2%
Provide Alternative Activities	1%	3%	2%
Deal with the Underlying Problems	1%	2%	2%
Teach Moderation	0%	3%	2%

(Sixty-six percent of those surveyed answered this question. The percentages are of those who answered. Survey does not contain all answers given.)

Source: The 1986 *CAMPUS LIFE* survey of high school students.

Here are some of the solutions students offered:

"I think scare tactics help" (Male, 16, Missouri).

"All they do at my school is preach and after a while it gets to the point where you just turn them off. I think you should just let people know about the problem, but stop preaching" (Female, 17, Montana).

"Start educating people. When I took health and biology, we just skipped over drug and alcohol abuse" (Male, 18, Texas).

"Have a required course on the effects of drugs and alcohol" (Female, 15, Missouri).

"School officials aren't accomplishing anything. They should help instead of punish" (Female, 17, Michigan).

"I think speakers who have experienced drug and alcohol abuse should come and talk to the students" (Female, 16, Michigan).

"I don't think the drug education program is working here. I still see the same burnouts selling drugs every day. I think we need to persuade people who haven't tried drugs not to start, and get counseling for the people who are really hooked" (Female, 16, Michigan).

"Stress prevention" (Male, 17, Missouri).

"Make people realize they have a problem" (Female, 16, Texas).

"I feel there should be a school-associated group for teens trying to get away from drugs and alcohol or problems associated with them" (Female, 15, Nevada).

"Teach why life would be better without drugs and alcohol" (Female, 14, Texas).

"I think that when adults catch children or people under eighteen using drugs, they deal with it the wrong way. They need help, not punishment" (Female, 15, Washington).

"More should be done to help teens who use drugs. Like support groups and rehab centers. And it shouldn't cost so much. And it should be more accessible. I have a relative who went to a rehab center and wasn't helped at all. He was then sent somewhere else and his parents had to pay over $15,000. People can't always afford it, therefore, many cases are not properly treated" (Male, 16, Ohio).

"I think public schools should have guest speakers at least once a year to talk to the student body about the short-term and long-term effects of using drugs and alcohol. These guest speakers should be people the students can relate to, like parents whose sons or daughters have abused. They should tell how it has affected the entire family" (Male, 16, Washington).

"I think that more people should start teaching kids in elementary school about how bad drugs and alcohol are, because that's when most of the kids start using. The kids should know the facts about drugs and alcohol. If they are scared by these facts, maybe they will not turn to substance abuse in the future. There should also be more advertising of hot line numbers to encourage more kids to seek help" (Female, 16, California).

"I think all high schools and colleges should have what my school has: an alternative club. It is a club of kids who know how to have fun without drinking and taking drugs. People in this club go to junior high and elementary schools and talk to kids about drugs and drinking—they talk about looking for things to do besides drinking and using drugs" (Female, 17, Virginia).

"Many kids (including myself) don't understand all the things that can happen when you take drugs or drink alcohol. If there were more education on the topic, then students wouldn't have to use drugs and alcohol out of curiosity" (Female, 15, Michigan).

"Be tough" (Female, 17, Texas).

"There needs to be better communication between students and teachers" (Male, 17, Texas).

"At the elementary level there is a wide-spread effort with the "Just Say No" group. At the high school and middle school level, there is not as much effort to reach people. I think the school should try to reach the older students more" (Female, 15, Texas).

"The anonymous programs [AA, for example] work because they involve honesty, trust, and fellowship. In those kinds of groups you deal with what caused you to drink in the first place" (Female, 17, Texas).

"Our school has started putting up posters in the halls showing the victims of drunken driving. I think that has been much more effective than threats. My friends and I have started thinking twice before we drive and drink" (Female, 17, Texas).

"The program at my school is mainly just statistics. It doesn't really get in-depth about drugs" (Female, 17, Nebraska).

"I think people who try to help other people with drug/alcohol problems need to realize that someone who's addicted needs first of all love, then they need to realize that no one can break free of a habit unless and until she wants to!! All we can do for them is help them and support them" (Female, 17, Oregon).

"Kids just make a lot of fun of the drug program here. I think the teachers should try to relate more to the students' level—use music, etc." (Female, 16, Ohio).

"If young people are involved in a church, their church needs to give a Christian viewpoint on drugs and alcohol" (Female, 17, Georgia).

"In our school the people who are in the "Just Say No" group do drugs. It's like a big hypocrisy. You need people who are really serious about it" (Female, 16, Texas).

"I wish these subjects would come out into the open more so kids would realize that it's not a have-to thing. They have a choice in the matter. Most teenagers are influenced by peer pressure and they need to know that they don't need friends like that" (Female, 16, Georgia).

"I think what aggravates students is that famous people talk on TV and say not to use drugs. And these people are always pointing to peer pressure as the main problem. They really don't know what they're talking about. Students want to talk to people who have used drugs or those who are still druggies. You just can't relate with people who have never been there. Nonusers have no idea what it's like, and it's impossible to try to figure out what it's like to do drugs and alcohol if you've never been there" (Female, 16, Ohio).

"For people who are in drug rehabilitation, they should show horrible films about what happens to drug addicts" (Female, 16, Missouri).

"I think what works best is to talk to people your age" (Male, 17, Texas).

"I think my school system should start having a required class on drugs and alcohol. I think it would help everybody a lot" (Female, 16, Minnesota).

"Drug education programs are too accusing" (Female, 17, Missouri).

"Most drug education programs are boring. You lose track of what the person is talking about. I don't think people pay attention anyway. The next day they're out partying again" (Female, 17, Missouri).

"The current drug programs aren't good because there are too many people telling you not to do something. By laws of human nature, everyone out there will do it" (Male, 15, Missouri).

"I think [the answer is] really showing these kids how they're destroying themselves and then providing an alternative—like Jesus Christ" (Female, 17, Texas).

"More young people need to get involved. It needs to get on a more personal level" (Female, 17, Texas).

TESTING

There has been much said on the pros and cons of drug screening programs. A 1986 Gallup survey indicated that teenagers approved of such programs for themselves and for others. It is humorously predictable that teenagers voiced the strongest approval of drug testing for teachers (88 percent)—placing them just slightly ahead of airline pilots (84 percent), police officers (83 percent) and members of the military (80 percent). However, what seems a bit unusual is that more students approved of drug testing for themselves (74 percent) than approved of drug testing for athletes (58 percent).

Some high school students from Illinois offer these opinions regarding drug testing for employees:

"I think companies should have mandatory drug testing. I would feel better knowing that a worker is supporting his or her family, rather than a drug or alcohol habit" (Female, 16).

CHART 6 APPROVAL OF DRUG TESTING PROGRAMS

Percent who approve of tests for each category

	National	Male	Female	Ages 13-15	Ages 16-18
High School Teachers	88%	85%	91%	89%	87%
Airline Pilots	84%	85%	83%	84%	84%
Police Officers	83%	83%	83%	84%	81%
Members of the Armed Services	80%	78%	82%	81%	80%
High School Students	74%	68%	79%	81%	66%
Professional Athletes	58%	58%	59%	62%	55%

Source: THE GALLUP YOUTH SURVEY (1986). Used by permission from the Associated Press.

"No, I don't agree with drug testing. I think if they want to use drugs on their own time, let them do it" (Male, 18).

"Yes to drug testing. It's a way to see if a person really is an addict" (Male, 15).

"No. It's your business what you do with your life and health. As long as you do your job right, it's nobody's business what 'private' things you do" (Female, 17).

"The only reason you should be testing for drugs is if drug use would interfere with the job you have to do" (Male, 16).

"I agree with drug testing. If someone has a problem with drugs or alcohol it can hurt the company he works for. He may come to work feeling really out of it. Then he can't do his job the way he should" (Female, 17).

"Yes, I think there should be mandatory drug testing. Someone may be high and an innocent person's life may be in danger because of it" (Male, 16).

"I think there should be testing only for the ones that employers think may be doing drugs" (Male, 16).

"Drug testing imposes on personal rights. People should be able to do what they want" (Male, 16).

"Yes. Drug testing would solve the drug problem" (Female, 16).

"No. It's nobody else's business" (Male, 16).

"Drug testing would help to know which people use drugs and which people don't" (Female, 16).

"Yes. I believe there should be drug testing. Drug use could affect the way a product is made. Like if an auto worker put a car together wrong, the buyer could risk injury or getting killed" (Male, 16).

Getting Tough?

The desire to enforce drug testing may be an indication of a "get tough" mood among students. I discovered a growing impatience with a perceived "softness" in dealing with drug abusers. One fifteen-year-old girl from Texas says bluntly, "Arrest them!" Others, a lesser number, felt a need not to punish, but help. "I don't think punishment is the answer in most cases," says a sixteen-year-old girl from Minnesota. "Usually the student who has drugs in school has a problem and should be referred to a counselor for treatment." What follows are several answers to the question, "What should your school do when a student is caught with drugs or alcohol?":

"I think the person who is caught should be taken to counseling" (Female, 15, Ohio).

"Punish them and put them in juvenile detention" (Female, 16, Texas).

"I think they should be sent to alcohol and drug meetings" (Female, 17, Wisconsin).

"I think students should be punished so that they won't do it again. Most people after being suspended go right back and do it again" (Female, 16, Ohio).

"Suspend them and give them an F for everything they missed while they were suspended" (Male, 15, Washington).

"Get them out and turn them over to the police" (Female, 16, South Dakota).

"Get them help at a rehabilitation center" (Female, 16, Ohio).

"I feel they have a right to explain. If their explanation isn't good enough, expel them from school" (Female, 15, Ohio).

"Have a serious discussion with their parents and put them in rehabilitation if needed" (Male, 15, Washington).

"Suspend them!" (Female, 16, Minnesota).

"The school should help them, not punish them. A person caught will not be benefited by being pushed out the door. Counseling and a good rehabilitation center are the best things" (Female, 17, Minnesota).

"Give them a criminal record" (Male, 16, Washington).

"In-school therapy" (Female, 17, South Dakota).

"Send them to a place where druggies are treated" (Female, 14, Washington).

"For one thing, just don't kick them out. That doesn't seem to do any good. Have a program at school and make them attend. You should also call the parents and have a meeting with the family" (Female, 15, Washington).

"The student should be punished" (Female, 16, Ohio).

"I think drug cases should be dealt with by the police. Alcohol cases should be handled by the school in a manner in which a student can be helped and not punished" (Male, 16, New York). (I found the last quote particularly interesting in light of the distinction this person makes between drug abusers and alcohol abusers: Punish the druggie, help the alcohol abuser.)

CAN ANYTHING REALLY BE DONE?

The low number of students offering solutions and the widely varied solutions given may show a growing pessimism among students. A few students I talked to stared blankly when I asked, "What can be done?" On the surveys many expressed their lack of hope:

"Leave us alone. Let us figure it out on our own" (Female, 16, Montana).

"No matter what you do, people will use drugs and alcohol" (Female, 15, Montana).

"Alcohol abuse cannot be stopped, drugs can be reduced by reducing availability. But alcohol can be gotten so easily" (Female, 17, Texas).

"This may surprise some people, but all these commercials that say, 'Yeah, it's OK to say no,' don't help" (Female, 15, Minnesota).

"One student I know of in a drug program went through treatment twice and still used drugs afterward" (Male, 16, Missouri).

"The illegal use of drugs is just like any other crime, and we have yet to stop murders, burglaries, etc." (Male, 15, Ohio).

"There's really nothing education can do, smart kids get addicted also" (Male, 16, Michigan).

"I know people who have sat and snorted cocaine while watching 'Don't Use Drugs' commercials. I think TV is wasting its money" (Female, 16, Missouri).

"You can tell horror stories until you're blue in the face and a person won't stop until she wants to" (Female, 16, Texas).

"The efforts to stop drug abuse are so weak that they aren't noticeable" (Male, 17, Michigan).

"I think it is great that people are fighting this issue, but I really think it's going to be impossible to completely defeat" (Female, 15, Ohio).

"There's nothing anyone can do about alcohol use among teenagers, and it's a shame. No matter what people do to keep kids from drinking, they can always get it" (Female, 16, Wisconsin).

"I've always wanted to help get people off drugs, but as yet I haven't found a way" (Female, 17, Georgia).

"Most people think that the 'Just Say No' campaign is a joke" (Male, 14, Texas).

From Pessimism to Healthy Realism

Bystanders and casual users of alcohol tend to be the most pessimistic about the drug problem. They often seem negative about the situation and certainly unwilling to get involved in finding solutions. Male bystanders also are the most willing to suggest harsh legal measures.

On the other hand, problem solvers or potential problem solvers usually take a longer, deeper look at the issues behind the issue. They ask, "Why is this person using?" As for solutions, they focus heavily on friendships, relationships, family, and a healthy self-esteem. While they may be a bit too optimistic in terms of short-term solutions, they usually are realistic about human nature. They have a sincere strain of compassion that is invariably missing in bystanders and in most casual drinkers. Problem solvers and potential problem solvers see beyond the "druggie" label to the hurting individual within.

Here are some areas that problem solvers and potential problem solvers feel need to be addressed to offer effective prevention and rehabilitation programs:

Compassion, openness, and honesty. If the counselor or educator takes a condemning, judgmental approach, the abuser will not feel like opening up. Also, if the educator or counselor is not honest about his or her own abuse, the abuser or struggling abuser will rarely respect the counsel of this person. Real problem solvers are those who are trustworthy, authentic, and empathetic.

"There must be an absolute openness and a caring environment. I think teenagers have a lot of areas in their lives that lead to drug and alcohol abuse, and a good drug program must help them work on all of these problems. I also think group therapy would help so they'd know they're not alone" (Female, 15, Texas).

"Caring is the best way to solve this huge social problem" (Male, 16, South Dakota).

Self-respect. Says one sixteen-year-old guy from Texas: "I used drugs and alcohol because it was hip, and I felt very pressured to do so. It wasn't until I had confidence in myself and understood my purpose in life that I didn't feel compelled to do drugs and drink alcohol." Self-respect, self-esteem, and self-confidence are essential in breaking loose

174 THE SEARCH FOR ANSWERS THAT WORK

from the pressures to drink and do drugs. And those elements must be present in successful drug and alcohol programs. The recognition of this need is expressed by the following students:

"Talk to abusers and try to build some self-respect and esteem" (Female, 17, Missouri).

"Build the abuser's confidence as an individual" (Female, 15, Missouri).

"We need to let kids know they can be liked just the way they are without getting drunk" (Female, 15, Washington).

"If teenagers weren't so insecure, they wouldn't do drugs. Teenagers need to learn how to feel secure, so they won't feel a need for drugs" (Female, 17, Texas).

Peer pressure. Peer pressure is much more subtle than arm-twisting. It affects all members of society, young and old. It affects adults when they "just feel" they have to drive a certain kind of car. It affects teenage guys when they walk into a room and have their hair fixed differently from all the other guys. It affects teenage girls when they want to look like the model in an ad. Peer pressure permeates all of culture and often moves us (sometimes unconsciously) to do certain things. But it's not always bad.

Peer pressure can be used positively. When groups of students decide against drug use and abuse, it often can have a positive effect on a school. Says a seventeen-year-old girl from Texas: "Peer pressure is strong in moving people to use drugs. Maybe the same pressure could stop them from using drugs."

Peer counseling, caring friends. There has been a growing stress on peers helping peers through crisis situations. It has been found effective for students with drug problems. It must be stressed, however, that this is not professional counseling. Some counseling professionals and religious leaders prefer to refer to this as "caring friends helping friends." This is helpful, but someone with severe drug problems needs professional therapy and possibly long-term rehabilitation efforts.

However, friends helping friends with drug or alcohol problems can have a tremendous impact in building self-esteem and giving incentives to avoid use. Peer counseling is most effective when it is preventative. In some schools, older students are paired with younger students in a positive modeling role. Before the younger student is introduced to drugs or alcohol, the older, positive role model can do much to influence that person away from drug or alcohol abuse.

Here are some students who stress friendship building as a solution to drug or alcohol use:

"I think it's important to show abusers that you're their friends and that you will be there when they need you" (Male, 16, Michigan).

"I think the best way for a drug and alcohol program to help people is through friends talking to friends" (Male, 15, Michigan).

"People who use drugs need more help than a drug, they need you" (Female, 17, Washington).

Early education. Several students I talked to are actively involved in giving drug and alcohol free programs for grade school students. Many students feel that prevention measures must begin in the elementary grades:

"Try to get to students in the lower grades. Help them to enjoy themselves and feel they have the self-worth to go drug free" (Male, 15, Michigan).

"If you really want to stop drugs, stop peer pressure at an early age. Teach self-respect before the damage is done" (Female, 15, Michigan).

"Start educating kids in the lower grades; show them the facts and statistics. Maybe then kids will realize they don't need it. They can build a stronger self-image and learn to say no" (Female, 17, Michigan).

The importance of family. The importance of parental involvement was expressed in this way:

"Maybe the kids who are drinking and taking drugs do this just to get attention from their parents. If these teenagers were encouraged to talk with their parents and just ask them to spend a little more time with them, maybe that would help these kids to work through their problems and their worries" (Female, 14, Texas).

"I think the drug user's family should be involved in any therapy that is done" (Female, 14, Missouri).

"Keeping away from drugs should start in the home at a young age" (Female, 14, Washington).

"I think that good parents should be able to talk to their sons and daughters frequently about the good and bad in society. Parents should be understanding, because the future of their children depends on them" (Female, 16, California).

"Drugs and alcohol are things that have gone on for many years. Parents should realize that their children may be involved. Awareness of parents is very important" (Female, 16, California).

"My advice to parents is: Build your child's self-esteem so that a low self-esteem won't drag your son or daughter down without a fight" (Female, 15, South Carolina).

"I feel that parents need to be taught to teach their children how to have good, clean fun. Children need to know that there are better ways of leading a happy, successful life than drinking and using drugs" (Female, 18, Oregon).

"I have a real smart dad who knows what is best for me, because he cares a lot. For example, I liked this guy, but I found out that he drinks. When I told my dad, he wouldn't let me go out with this guy because he knows I might get hurt. And I wouldn't want to hurt my dad by going against his will" (Female, 19, Michigan).

"I feel that teenagers who have parental support don't get into as much trouble. Their parents care about them and what they do. When parents don't care, the kids don't care" (Female, 15, Wisconsin).

Alternatives. Many students complain about boredom and lack creativity in finding things to do besides drink and use drugs. Others seek alternatives only to find that these alternatives are not readily accepted. Many students are especially resistant to alternative programs set up by adults. One drug-free program in Chicago is a well-advertised failure. Part of the problem with these programs, critics speculate, is that students are not a part of the planning.

If an alternative is going to work, activities must be well organized and students must be the chief motivators and planners. There must also be long-term goals. One-shot "alcohol free" parties don't make it over the long haul. (In fact, in one case I heard of, kids showed up at a "alcohol free" party thinking they would get free alcohol.)

The next section presents comments from several students who have found alternatives to the drug and alcohol scene.

PROJECT 714: A POSITIVE MODEL FOR ACTION

When I boarded the plane at Chicago's Midway Airport for the South, I had my doubts. Could this project really be as effective as they claimed? Or was it just another one of those "good ideas" largely created, run, and attended by adults?

Upon arriving at Project 714 headquarters in Chattanooga, Tennessee, I was handed several slickly produced brochures and booklets proclaiming such things as, "Giving the teens in your schools a fighting chance against drugs," and "Win the battle against drug abuse in your community." As I read the material, it all made good, common sense.

Schools were challenged to get involved; positive peer pressure was held up as an effective solution; student, parent, and school involvement was trumpeted; friends helping friends served as the main model for positive change. Project 714 stressed prevention as the key to solving the teenage drug and alcohol problem while also offering services and support groups for struggling abusers and for students who have abuse present in the home.

When I met the adult leaders of Project 714, I was told some pretty impressive facts:

- Active since the early '80s, this high school-based, peer-oriented program claims to have involved 11,000 teenagers from Chattanooga, Nashville, and northern Georgia.
- In rural Hamilton County (Georgia), Project 714 claims to involve 64 percent of all high school students. Most of these students are members of Students Staying Straight (Triple S), a club stressing abstinence from both drugs and alcohol.
- Many administrators claim Project 714 is responsible for declines in drug and alcohol use both on and off the high school campus.

To explain the success, Jimmy Lee, Project 714 founder and president, told me, "An effective program requires more than just giving out bumper stickers and buttons. There has to be somebody in there working with kids on a day-to-day basis."

Anthony Otey, the full-time, day-to-day coordinator of the program's adult staff, reinforced his boss's perspective: "Everyone talks about the drug problem. Drugs don't have problems; people have problems. In our country we've used a lot of methods: drug education, scare tactics, and moral or value clarification. Some kids can be educated, some kids can be scared out of use, some can be moralized. But none of those is going to work by itself. No one way works, except love."

Otey went on to stress the need to get beneath the surface to the deeper problems of abusers and potential abusers. He also stressed community-wide involvement and "ownership" of the program, bringing together school administrators, teachers, parents, and local businesses: "Project 714 brings all these people together and says, 'The kids need our help.' So when we have a drug-free activity, the local skating rink may open up its facility to us free of charge. Parents don't just drop their kids off, but take time to cook hot dogs with them. It gets the community involved in the process."

At the core of the program's success, Otey stressed, is the commitment of students: "Many young people wanted to be identified in a positive way for their views on drugs and alcohol. They wanted to start a group where kids were committed to staying straight, where it's not cool to use drugs."

The students came up with a club name—Students Staying Straight (Triple S)—and developed specific club guidelines. They also drew up a contract which would be signed by all club members declaring abstinence from drugs and alcohol. They decided to hold regular meetings where speakers would discuss drug and alcohol abuse. The students set up drug and alcohol free activities that were open to the entire school. All of those aspects were incorporated into the program, along with membership cards, a handbook, and Students Staying Straight T-shirts.

After our discussion, Otey and I began our rounds to several schools involved in Project 714. Triple S bulletin boards appeared in all of the schools we visited. Stapled to most of those boards were the complete listings of Triple S club members. One guidance counselor who helps with the Triple S program at her school told me that the list of names serves as a monitoring device. If students aren't sticking by their contracts, if they aren't abstaining from drugs and alcohol, fellow students are the first to know. So peer pressure, positive peer pressure, is at work.

But the most significant indications of the program's success were the conversations I had with students.

Jack[1]: "Honesty Is Really Important"
Jack had come from a family where drug and alcohol abuse was present and even encouraged. In the face of suspension from school for on-campus drug use, Jack chose the other option: becoming involved in Project 714's Chemical Awareness group, the program for struggling abusers. Involved in the program for more than a year when I met him, he was still suffering from some of the long-term effects of his abuse: slurred speech, short attention span, loss of memory, and a devastated self-worth. Yet Jack has been making positive forward steps. Through his support group, led by his adult supervisor, he has been learning the importance of honesty and openness with other struggling abusers in the group.

While I talked with Jack, his teacher/supervisor sat in. I was continually impressed by her interest and compassion for him. When he

[1]All names have been changed.

seemed unable to think of something to say, she offered him words of encouragement. Here was an adult offering needed input and role modeling. Because of the supervisor's involvement in the interview, I have chosen to quote her along with Jack in a question-and-answer format.

Tell me about the experience that led up to your abuse.

Jack: My Dad was a hippie from the sixties and kept right on using after he got married. One time, when I was about five or six, I saw him smoking pot and so I went over and took a joint from him and started smoking myself. I started smoking pot and drinking a lot at a pretty young age; I did some acid and I started doing mushrooms and stuff like that. By high school I was firing up heroin.

Did you hang around with friends who also used?

Jack: So-called friends.

Why do you say that?

Jack: They're not really your friends if they get high with you, because they don't care nothing about you. People who do drugs are using each other, that's why I call them so-called friends.

Why did you continue to do drugs over the past several years?

Jack: To get high. It makes you feel good. But eventually it stopped feeling good.

What would you say to somebody who says, "I enjoy doing drugs. I like doing drugs. I don't have any problems created by doing drugs"?

Jack: I would just tell them that they will pay for it in the long run, because they are abusing their body.

Supervisor: They have to be at a point where they want to stop. They won't quit unless they are at that point where they know there are going to be negative consequences.

Jack: Last year they talked to me and I wasn't ready to stop.

Supervisor: No, last year Jack wasn't ready to talk or stop. He's come a long way in the past year. The consequences weren't bad enough for him to stop. He had no negative consequences.

What negative consequences finally changed things, Jack?

Jack: I did some crack and it scared me. I thought I was going to die. I don't want to talk about that.

Tell me about your involvement with the Chemical Awareness group.

Jack: Last year after I got suspended for having drugs on campus, they put me in the group to help me.

Supervisor: See, students caught on campus with drugs can't come back to school unless they join the Chemical Awareness group. These students sign a contract when they come back saying they will abstain for nine weeks from the use of any chemicals or alcohol. Each week, when they get to group, we ask them, "Did you keep the contract?" Anything that is said in group is kept in confidence. Obviously, a lot of times they would lie to you at first. But eventually, as the students in group develop a closeness, they begin monitoring each other. They begin to point out when another person is lying. I must add that it has not been easy getting to this point. When we first started Jack's Chemical Awareness group last year, I thought it was the biggest waste of time I could possibly imagine. We got nowhere with the kids. We couldn't get a trust level going.

Jack, what were your impressions at that time?

Jack: Yeah, it seemed like a big waste of time. That was the first part of the year, before I got scared from the crack. Then it hit me that I needed to do something. So I got serious about it in the last part of this past year.

Supervisor: We had made some of them quit near the end of the year. They would just laugh and they'd be silly and goofy and then we wouldn't let them come. After a couple of months, they wanted to come back. And when they came back they had a different perspective. But that was near the end of last year. I don't think those kids, and that included Jack, had enough time to build trust. Time is really important. This year is just a whole different story.

Why do you think that is the case?

Supervisor: A lot of them weren't at that point where they were ready to quit using drugs. In Jack's situation, he had a bad experience and I think it really made him look at things. Jack's not perfect yet, but if you could have seen him last year and then see him now, he is a totally different person. He was just completely out of it last year. He did the craziest things. He was very disruptive in class.

This year he's gotten an A in Spanish, he's good in math—although he still has trouble with some of his subjects and he probably always will have trouble. But you know, he's functioning, he's sensitive to other people. It's just really neat to see him emerge as a person. I knew he was always there but I couldn't get to him through that cloud.

Jack: Last year I wasn't ready for group. I didn't really know myself then.

Tell me about a typical group meeting.

Jack: We meet once a week to talk about what we did between each meeting. We look at each other and decide who is lying and who is telling the truth. If we think someone is lying, we'll confront him with it. Honesty is really the most important part of our group.

Mark: "You Have to Practice What You Preach"

Before I met with Mark I had the opportunity to talk with his adult sponsor. When she told me about Mark, I could tell she respected him for his intelligence, honesty, overall friendliness, and progress in fighting his abuse. Most of all I could tell she respected him as an individual. As I met with staff involved in successful programs, that one characteristic came through again and again: respect for the individual. I rarely sensed a naiveté about the abuser's negative traits. Instead I sensed a desire to scrape off the labels and see each person as an individual.

Mark was already profiled in chapter 3 (see page 82 for biographical information). Having been through therapy and as a regular attender of AA, Mark has shown strong progress. He currently helps lead meetings. It is important to note the differences between Jack and Mark; it is a demonstration of the slow yet progressive nature of the successful rehabilitation process. It also demonstrates the importance of networking a variety of counseling and help services.

I had been in therapy for my own drug abuse for some time when the adult sponsor of the Chemical Awareness group came around to the different classes. After giving a short talk, she asked if anybody was interested in being involved and I told her I was. Since I had been in drug treatment, I felt I knew a little about what was going on. I thought it would be good to have support here at school. I also thought maybe I had something to offer the other kids who were still struggling a lot with abuse. See, this wasn't a situation where I was forced to join group; I was currently off drugs. Actually, our group is unlike a lot of Chemical Awareness groups because the kids involved are mainly there voluntarily.

Right now, I am real satisfied with the progress everybody is mak-

ing in our group. I try very hard to be the best help I can. Sometimes I have to get a little tough, in a loving way. If somebody isn't being up-front and honest I'll call him on it. It's pretty easy for me to tell when somebody is hiding something because not long ago I was doing the same thing. We're getting some things done. More than I expected.

I got involved with group because I am currently at step twelve in AA: helping other people who have the same problem I have. Actually, helping other people helps me more than I could ever help them.

My involvement has really been good for my entire family. See, my dad, who went in for alcohol treatment a year before I did, under-went counseling with me. Much of our counseling also involved the entire family. Before we had counseling the whole family fought all the time. Now that my dad and I are straight, my mom and little sis-ter, who haven't ever abused, are even different people. They're much happier. We all talk a lot now. As a matter of fact, we talk so much I bet an outsider coming into the room would want to put ear-plugs in his ears. I really think the family wars we used to have are over. It's so good to be able to sit down and have a discussion without getting into an argument.

If I've learned one thing through it all, I've learned that drugs and alcohol are no way to escape pain. Sure, I'd like to have all of my problems solved instantly. But life doesn't work that way. It takes time; you have to work it out over the long haul.

There's just no way I would want to go back to my old way. It's nothing but a waste. Plus, I really want to influence others to stay off drugs and find a better way to live their lives. If I drank even one beer, I'd become a hypocrite. If I did that, it'd be like saying, "I can do it [drink], but you can't." You have to practice what you preach.

Students who had been in AA often mentioned to me Mark's point about helping others. School programs like Project 714 offer a good out-let for such service, and allow the former abuser to take the focus off of himself and put it onto others. It allows him to demonstrate his changed perspective before his peers. Thus he is able to put positive peer pressure to work, which results in a growing self-respect as he discovers that he is needed and appreciated. Certainly, Mark's experience of reaching out has been positive and life-stretching.

Like the other students involved in Project 714, Mark received not only encouragement and support, but education. Along with bringing expert speakers on drug and alcohol abuse into the school, Project 714 sends students to seminars provided by PRIDE, Parents' Resource Institute for Drug Education. Offering resources drawn from the latest research, PRIDE is widely respected and serves as an informal type of networking for many school-based drug and alcohol programs across the country. Networking with professional resource banks, like PRIDE, helps local programs avoid misinformation and build credibility.

Margo: "See the Bigger Picture"

Margo, slender and pert, wore an oversized black-and-yellow letter jacket and a class ring affixed, rubber-band style, to a ring finger. She bubbled with those qualities present in a school's most popular students. But unlike many who roam with the usual in-crowd, Margo chose the crowd who thinks smart kids don't use drugs and alcohol. An officer in her school's Triple S club, Margo starts her comments by stating the goals of Triple S.

Our main goal is to show that there really are a lot of kids out there not using drugs and alcohol. It's just not true that everybody is doing it. And I know for a fact that there are friends out there who accept you for who you are and not what you do.

I became involved with Triple S last year, my first year in high school. In the middle school, I was running with older kids and doing things I shouldn't have been doing, like drinking. When I started high school, I found out about Triple S and thought it would give me a chance to get with more people who didn't drink. I really didn't think drinking was that exciting; it didn't thrill me. I just didn't know there was anybody who didn't do it. Triple S showed me that there were many kids who kept themselves straight.

As the group's current vice president, I work with the other officers to get more people involved. We help bring speakers in for school assemblies. We often have speakers who have used drugs, but have changed. These people talk about their pasts and why they now feel using and drinking is wrong. Obviously, there are some students at these all-school meetings who don't want to be there, but I just hope they learn something.

We also have a lot of smaller activities for anybody who wants to come. We have weekend lock-ins, we sponsor dances, and we try to get ideas from the group about what they want to do. One big thing we do is go to PRIDE in Atlanta. It's an international conference against drug abuse. It's really great. It would be neat if you could take everybody. We also have meetings just for Triple S members. It's our way to get together and show support for each other.

Joining Triple S isn't just a set of guidelines and rules. It's so much more than that. Saying you'll abstain is just your way of demonstrating your values. After people sign contracts, some will come back and say, "I can keep the contract during the week, but I can't keep it on weekends." And we just say, "You know, we're not going to spy on you. It's how you value yourself. When you sign that contract you're making a commitment to yourself. If you don't keep the contract, you're hurting your own body, your own life. In the long run it's going to be not only yourself you hurt. You're going to hurt your family and your friends."

While Triple S members may have friends who will put them down for not using, they also have friends who will accept them for who they are. We let them know that we are here to build up their confidence in themselves.

There are a lot of kids who don't want to use drugs and alcohol, and there are a lot of kids who use just because they think they have to because they're with their friends. You have to learn how to stand up for yourself and hold your own ground. It's hard. It's really hard. There are a lot of times when you have pressure put on you. Even as an officer, I have people coming around pressuring me, wanting me to get involved in drugs and alcohol.

For me it helps to try to see the bigger picture. I am not only responsible for myself. I am responsible for others as well. I really think older kids need to see that they have responsibility for younger kids. It bothers me that kids in the fifth and sixth grades start drinking because they see the older kids doing it. Older kids are supposed to be their role models, but they often aren't. The older kids often think it's funny to watch the younger kids drink.

High school students need to realize the responsibility they have for others. They must learn to have enough respect for themselves to do what they feel is right.

The following traits are what make Margo an effective problem solver in her high school:

Active. Margo isn't satisfied to sit on the sidelines, to be a bystander. She is aggressively involved with talking to others about Triple S, and she seeks to help offer creative ways to get others involved.

Not alone. Margo doesn't do her work in a vacuum. She takes time to brainstorm ideas with other students. She's open to explore new ideas.

Aware of the big picture. Margo is able to see beyond herself to how her abuse could affect others. She feels a responsibility for setting a good example for younger people. Even casual use of alcohol could under-mine her ability to fulfill that responsibility. Role modeling is extremely important to her.

Willing to share. She talks about her responsibility to friends and fam-ily. One abuser affects many other people. And to Margo, one abstainer/problem solver also affects (or should affect) many other people in a positive way.

Has self-respect and peer influence. Margo has a healthy understand-ing of peer influence and self-respect. Before students can break from negative peer influence, they must feel good about themselves. Margo is strong in stressing inner values and a respect for oneself as the chief means for avoiding negative peer pressure.

Realistic. Margo knows change must be long-term and there will be times of failure. While some kids cheat on their Triple S contracts, she understands that change comes one step at a time.

Educated. Talking with Margo, I discovered that she "knows her stuff" about drugs and alcohol. Before someone can help others, he must have a good understanding of the issues involved in drug and alco-hol abuse.

Enjoys life. Margo's lively personality and upbeat attitude tell me that she is not missing a thing by abstaining. That fact in itself could influ-ence others to become involved in Triple S.

Jenny: "What Helps the Most Is Role Modeling"

A curly-headed blonde with sparkling blue eyes, Jenny blends in well with the other preppy dressers in her high school. She's a friendly girl who greeted me with a polite handshake. She and her high school friends prefer the positive peer approach: "When I'm at a party where kids are drinking, I don't start preaching and getting down on them for what they are doing. I've found that confronting them in a negative way doesn't work. But if they can see me drinking my Coke and having a good time anyway, they may feel that they don't need alcohol."

Her friendly, upbeat attitude can't help but impress the kids at the grade schools where she often talks about drug and alcohol abuse. Dur-ing our interview we focused mainly on her interactions with those ele-mentary students.

*Last year there were about eight of us from my high school who went
around to different elementary schools. We would talk to the sixth
graders mainly—get them into a group and talk to them for as long
as the teachers would let us. Our programs usually lasted anywhere
from thirty minutes to an hour and a half. We would sit them down
and just start talking to them about drugs and alcohol. Our main goal
was to prepare them for what they are going to face in junior high
and high school. On the positive side, we wanted to let them know
that there is a Triple S club in junior high, and we wanted to challenge them to get involved.*

*One of the real effective things we do is have every other kid stand
up. Then one of us would say, "It's likely that this many of you are going to experience some kind of problem with drugs or alcohol." If you
just give them percentages, that slips right past them. But when you
have them stand up, they can see how big the problem really is. I
think this helps them to realize what they have to prepare for and why
it's so important to join with peers who want to stay straight.*

*After we get their attention through this kind of exercise, they open
up and will listen to what we have to say. We also have them ask us
questions. Sometimes I discover that these young kids know more
than I do about drugs and that's scary, because what they know is
usually the street kind of stuff—the stuff that attracts so many kids to
drugs and alcohol. What I think really helps kids the most is having
older teenagers, role models, standing in front of them and showing
by example that we believe it's good and fun to be straight. It helps a
lot more than having an adult just standing there and lecturing.*

*This next year we're planning on expanding what we do to include
a more fully developed program with skits and plays on how peer
pressure influences young people to drink and use drugs.*

THAT'S NOT ALL

By no means is Project 714 the only effective program. To help you see
what is going on nationwide, I will close this chapter with a few quotes
from students about current problem solving efforts:

"I feel that most teens go to parties and get drunk because there is
nothing else to do. There should be more places open for teens on weekend nights. We, the Quad cities, just opened a place called Stage 2. It's a
nonalcoholic bar, with Pepsi, pizza and chips, a dance floor, and a rec
and TV room" (Female, 17, Iowa).

"I guess you could say I know what it's like to have been there. I am an alcoholic—sober now for around a year. I want others to know what drugs and alcohol can do to your life. So I go around to junior high and elementary schools talking to kids about what abuse did to me. I like to think that I am helping others to avoid what I went through" (Male, 17, Illinois).

"I am involved in Youth Temperance Council and I am very proud of what this group is doing. YTC is a Christian-oriented interdenominational group with local, state, national, and world chapters. The motto of the council is, 'A good time with a purpose.' Through the council we hope to create positive peer pressure that will help others in their everyday lives. The pledge that is signed by all members reads: 'I promise, by the help of God, never to use alcoholic beverages, other narcotics, or tobacco, and to encourage everyone else to do the same.'

"I am really thankful that God brought such a group as this into my life. I am very excited about our ongoing plans to help others" (Female, 19, Illinois).

"We have an organization at our school that goes to grade schools and tells kids how to say no. Our schools aren't perfect yet, but we are trying in a positive way to stop drug abuse" (Female, 16, Missouri).

"At my school we have a group called Friends Reaching In Every Direction. And they teach a lot of people about drugs and alcohol" (Female, 15, Missouri).

"I'm in a Reach America program and I hope to help our community become drug free!" (Female, 16, Michigan).

"First of all, 'Substance Abuse' is a course that juniors and seniors may take at my high school. During the first half of the school year, students in this class learn about the effects of alcohol and drug abuse on the family. For the second half of the year, the students prepare lessons to teach to elementary classes.

"In addition to the substance abuse class, my school has a SADD chapter. Finally, once a year members of the junior class go on a weekend retreat called HUGS (Human Understanding and Growth Seminar). Although students are not required to attend this retreat, the vast majority do. At the retreat, students take part in large group sessions where a speaker talks about his or her own past abuse of alcohol or drugs. After this, students break up into small groups and discuss alcohol- and drug-related problems or issues.

"In my opinion, these programs are helping to fight and prevent drug problems in my town" (Female, 17, New York).

"I've had a lot of chances to talk in elementary schools about saying no to drug and alcohol abuse. And the response of the kids has been wonderful. We'd talk about specific situations in which they might be faced with a decision about drugs or drinking. And when I'd ask what they were going to do in that situation, they'd all scream in unison, 'Say No!' But then I'd tell them how they'd be called 'geeks,' 'chickens' and lots of other names if they didn't go along. How they'd sometimes feel left out. But then I'd also tell them they could do it.

"I'd always tell them how I'd gotten through ninth, tenth, eleventh, and twelfth grades and I'd never had to take a drink, smoke pot, or take drugs. And that never failed to impress them. So many of these little elementary school kids thought those things were just naturally a part of high school life. I made sure they knew it didn't have to be and they could be strong enough to say no" (Female, 18, Kansas).

"I am president of my school drug and alcohol free group, and the other officers and I have been focusing on three areas: 1) education; 2) peer leadership; 3) social activities. One of our dances drew up to 250 people. We hope that's helped people become aware of us and what we are doing and maybe caused some to think twice about their use of drugs and alcohol.

"We have also given some workshops for other high school students on the problems created by abuse and on how to set up a program like ours. While our program is fairly new, I think we're off to a good start" (Female, 17, Illinois).

"I'm involved in my school's group, Pirates Against Drunk Driving [named after the school's mascot]. Most of us involved are athletes. We hold dances and activities that are alcohol and drug free. I think it helps a lot of students think twice. And it's good for me because it helps me take a stand" (Male, 16, Colorado).

SPECIFIC DRUGS AND THEIR EFFECTS

The U.S. Department of Education offers the following information about drugs and their effects. While some terms and certain drugs are missing, this resource (published in 1986), offers the most up-to-date information at the time of the publication of *What Teenagers Are Saying about Drugs and Alcohol.*

CANNABIS/Effects

All forms of cannabis, including marijuana, have negative physical and mental effects. Several regularly observed physical effects of cannabis are a substantial increase in the heart rate, bloodshot eyes, a dry mouth and throat, and increased appetite.

Use of cannabis may impair or reduce short-term memory and comprehension, alter sense of time, and reduce ability to perform tasks requiring concentration and coordination (such as driving a car). Research also shows that students do not retain knowledge when they are "high." Motivation and cognition may be altered, making the acquisition of new information difficult. Marijuana can also produce paranoia and psychosis.

Because users often inhale the unfiltered smoke deeply and then hold it in their lungs as long as possible, marijuana is damaging to the lungs and pulmonary system. Marijuana smoke contains more cancer-causing agents than tobacco.

Long-term users of cannabis may develop psychological dependence and require more of the drug to get the same effect. The drug can become the center of their lives.

CHART 7

TYPE	WHAT IS IT CALLED?	WHAT DOES IT LOOK LIKE?	HOW IS IT USED?
Marijuana	Pot Grass Weed Reefer Dope Mary Jane Sinsemilla Acapulco Gold Thai Sticks	Dried parsley mixed with stems that may include seeds	Eaten Smoked
Tetrahydro-cannabinol	THC	Soft gelatin capsules	Taken orally Smoked
Hashish	Hash	Brown or black cakes or balls	Eaten Smoked
Hashish Oil	Hash Oil	Concentrated syrupy liquid varying in color from clear to black	Smoked— mixed with tobacco

INHALANTS/Effects

Immediate negative effects of inhalants include nausea, sneezing, coughing, nosebleeds, fatigue, lack of coordination, and loss of appetite. Solvents and aerosol sprays also decrease the heart and respiratory rates and impair judgment. Amyl and butyl nitrite cause rapid pulse, headaches, and involuntary passing of urine and feces. Long-term use may result in hepatitis or brain hemorrhage.

Deeply inhaling the vapors or using large amounts over a short period of time may result in disorientation, violent behavior, unconsciousness, or death. High concentrations of inhalants can cause suffocation by displacing the oxygen in the lungs or by depressing the central nervous system to the point that breathing stops.

Long-term use can cause weight loss, fatigue, electrolyte imbalance, and muscle fatigue. Repeated sniffing of concentrated vapors over time can permanently damage the nervous system.

CHART 8

TYPE	WHAT IS IT CALLED?	WHAT DOES IT LOOK LIKE?	HOW IS IT USED?
Nitrous Oxide	Laughing gas Whippets	Propellant for whipped cream in aerosol spray can Small 8-gram metal cylinder sold with a balloon or pipe (buzz bomb)	Vapors inhaled
Amyl Nitrite	Poppers Snappers	Clear yellowish liquid in ampules	Vapors inhaled
Butyl Nitrite	Rush Bolt Locker room Bullet Climax	Packaged in small bottles	Vapors inhaled
Chlorohydrocarbons	Aerosol sprays	Aerosol paint cans Containers of cleaning fluid	Vapors inhaled
Hydrocarbons	Solvents	Cans of aerosol propellants, gasoline, glue, paint thinner	Vapors inhaled

STIMULANT: COCAINE/Effects

Cocaine stimulates the central nervous system. Its immediate effects include dilated pupils and elevated blood pressure, heart rate, respiratory rate, and body temperature. Occasional use can cause a stuffy or runny nose, while chronic use can ulcerate the mucous membrane of the nose. Injecting cocaine with unsterile equipment can cause AIDS, hepatitis, and other diseases. Preparation of freebase, which involves the use of volatile solvents, can result in death or injury from fire or explosion. Cocaine can produce psychological and physical dependency, a feeling that the user cannot function without the drug. In addition, tolerance develops rapidly so that the user must continually increase the amount of drug used to get the desired effects.

Crack or freebase rock is extremely addictive, and its effects are felt within ten seconds. The physical effects include dilated pupils, increased pulse rate, elevated blood pressure, insomnia, loss of appetite, tactile hallucinations, paranoia, and seizures.

The use of cocaine can cause death by disrupting the brain's control of the heart and respiration.

CHART 9

TYPE	WHAT IS IT CALLED?	WHAT DOES IT LOOK LIKE?	HOW IS IT USED?
Cocaine	Coke Snow Flake White Blow Nose Candy Big C Snowbirds Lady	White crystalline powder, often diluted with other ingredients	Inhaled through nasal passages Injected Smoked
Crack or cocaine	Crack Freebase rocks Rock	Light brown or beige pellets or crystalline rocks that resemble coagulated soap: often packaged in small vials	Smoked

OTHER STIMULANTS/Effects

Stimulants can cause increased heart and respiratory rates, elevated blood pressure, dilated pupils, and decreased appetite. In addition, users may experience sweating, headache, blurred vision, dizziness, sleeplessness, and anxiety. Extremely high doses can cause a rapid or irregular heartbeat, tremors, loss of coordination, and even physical collapse.

CHART 10

TYPE	WHAT IS IT CALLED?	WHAT DOES IT LOOK LIKE?	HOW IS IT USED?

Amphet-amines	Speed
	Uppers
	Ups
	Black Beauties
	Pep Pills
	Copilots
	Bumblebees
	Hearts
	Benzedrine
	Drexedrine
	Footballs
	Biphetamine
		Capsules
		Pills
		Tablets
			Taken orally
			Injected
			Inhaled
			  through nasal
			  passages

Metham-phetamines	Crank
	Crystal Meth
	Crystal
	Methedrine
	Speed
		White powder
		Pills
		A rock which
		  resembles a
		  block of paraffin
			Taken orally
			Injected
			Inhaled
			  through nasal
			  passages

Additional Stimulants	Ritalin Cylert Preludin Didrex Pre-State Voranil Tenuate Tepanil Pondimin Sandrex Plegine Ionamin	Pills Capsules Tablets	Taken orally Injected

An amphetamine injection creates a sudden increase in blood pressure that can result in stroke, very high fever, or heart failure.

In addition to the physical effects, users report feeling restless, anxious, and moody. Higher doses intensify the effects. Persons who use large amounts of amphetamines over a long period of time can develop an amphetamine psychosis that includes hallucinations, delusions, and paranoia. These symptoms usually disappear when drug use ceases.

DEPRESSANTS/Effects

The effects of depressants are in many ways similar to the effects of alcohol. Small amounts can produce calmness and relaxed muscles, but somewhat larger doses can cause slurred speech, staggering gait, and altered perception. Very large doses can cause respiratory depression,

CHART 11

TYPE	WHAT IS IT CALLED?	WHAT DOES IT LOOK LIKE?	HOW IS IT USED?
Barbiturates	Downers Barbs Blue Devils Red Devils Yellow Jacket Yellows Nembutal Seconal Amytal Tuinals	Red, yellow, blue, or red and blue capsules	Taken orally
Methaqua-lone	Quaaludes Ludes Sopors	Tablets	Taken orally
Tranquil-izers	Valium Librium Equanil Miltown Serax Tranxene	Tablets Capsules	Taken orally

coma, and death. The combination of depressants and alcohol can multiply the effects of the drugs, thereby multiplying the risks.

The use of depressants can cause both physical and psychological dependence. Regular use over time may result in a tolerance to the drug, leading the user to increase the quantity consumed. When regular users suddenly stop taking large doses, they may develop withdrawal symptoms ranging from restlessness, insomnia, and anxiety to convulsions and death.

Babies born to mothers who abuse depressants during pregnancy may be physically dependent on the drugs and show withdrawal symptoms shortly after they are born. Birth defects and behavioral problems also may result.

HALLUCINOGENS/Effects

Phencyclidine (PCP) interrupts the functions of the neocortex, the section of the brain that controls the intellect and keeps instincts in check. Because the drug blocks pain receptors, violent PCP episodes may result in self-inflicted injuries.

The effects of PCP vary, but users frequently report a sense of distance and estrangement from their feelings. Time and body movement are slowed down. Muscular coordination worsens and senses are dulled. Speech is blocked and incoherent.

Chronic users of PCP report persistent memory problems and speech difficulties. Some of these effects may last six months to a year following prolonged daily use. Mood disorders, depression, anxiety, and violent behavior also occur. In later stages of chronic use, users often exhibit paranoid and violent behavior and experience hallucinations.

Large doses may produce convulsions and coma, heart and lung failure, or ruptured blood vessels in the brain.

Lysergic acid (LSD), mescaline, and psilocybin cause illusions and hallucinations. The physical effects may include dilated pupils, elevated body temperature, increased heart rate and blood pressure, loss of appetite, sleeplessness, and tremors.

Sensations and feelings may change rapidly. It is common to have a bad psychological reaction to LSD, mescaline, and psilocybin. The user may experience panic, confusion, suspicion, anxiety, and loss of control. Delayed effects, or flashbacks, can occur after use has ceased.

CHART 12

TYPE	WHAT IS IT CALLED?	WHAT DOES IT LOOK LIKE?	HOW IS IT USED?

Phencyclidine	PCP
	Angel Dust
	Loveboat
	Lovely
	Hog
	Killer Weed
		Liquid
		Capsules
		White crystalline
		  powder
		Pills
			Taken orally
			Injected
			Smoked (can
			  be sprayed
			  on ciga-
			  rettes, pars-
			  ley, and
			  marijuana)

Lysergic Acid Diethylamide	LSD
	Acid
	Green or Red
	  Dragon
	White Lightning
	Blue Heaven
	Sugar Cubes
	Microdot
		Brightly colored
		  tablets
		Impregnated blot-
		  ter paper
		Thin squares of
		  gelatin
		Clear liquid
			Taken orally
			Licked off
			  paper
			Gelatin and
			  liquid can be
			  put in the
			  eyes

Mescaline and Peyote	Mesc
	Buttons
	Cactus
		Hard brown discs
		Tablets
		Capsules
			Discs
			  (chewed,
			  swallowed,
			  or smoked)
			Tablets and
			  capsules
			  (taken orally)

Psilocybin	Magic
	  mushrooms
	Mushrooms
		Fresh or dried
		  mushrooms
			Chewed and
			  swallowed

NARCOTICS/Effects

Narcotics initially produce a feeling of euphoria that often is followed by drowsiness, nausea, and vomiting. Users also may experience constricted pupils, watery eyes, and itching. An overdose may produce slow and shallow breathing, clammy skin, convulsions, coma, and possibly death.

Tolerance to narcotics develops rapidly and dependence is likely. The use of contaminated syringes may result in diseases as AIDS, endocardi-

CHART 13

TYPE	WHAT IS IT CALLED?	WHAT DOES IT LOOK LIKE?	HOW IS IT USED?
Heroin	Smack Horse Brown Sugar Junk Mud Big H Black Tar	Powder, white to dark brown Tar-like substance	Injected Inhaled through nasal passages Smoked
Methadone	Dolophine Methadose Amidone	Solution	Taken orally Injected
Codeine	Empirin com- pound with Codeine Tylenol with Codeine Codeine in cough medicines	Dark liquid varying in thickness Capsules Tablets	Taken orally Injected
Morphine	Pectoral syrup	White crystals Hypodermic tablets Injectable solutions	Injected Taken orally Smoked
Meperidine	Pethidine Demerol Mepergan	White powder Solution Tablets	Taken orally Injected
Opium	Paregoric Dover's Powder Parepectolin	Dark brown chunks Powder	Smoked Eaten
Other Narcotics	Percocet Percodan Tussinex Fentanyl Darvon Talwin Lomotil	Tablets Capsules Liquid	Taken orally Injected

tis, and hepatitis. Addiction in pregnant women can lead to premature, stillborn, or addicted infants who experience severe withdrawal symptoms.

DESIGNER DRUGS/Effects

Illegal drugs are defined in terms of their chemical formulas. To circumvent these legal restrictions, underground chemists modify the molecular structure of certain illegal drugs to produce analogs known as

CHART 14

TYPE	WHAT IS IT CALLED?	WHAT DOES IT LOOK LIKE?	HOW IS IT USED?
Analogs of Fentanyl (Narcotic)	Synthetic Heroin China White	White powder resembling heroin	Inhaled through nasal passages Injected
Analogs of Meperidine (Narcotic)	Synthetic Heroin MPTP (New Heroin) MPPP PEPAP	White powder	Inhaled through nasal passages Injected
Analogs of Amphetamines and Methamphetamines (Hallucinogens)	MDMA (Ecstasy, XTC, Adam, Essence) MDM STP PMA 2, 5-DMA TMA DOM DOB	White powder Tablets Capsules	Taken orally Injected Inhaled through nasal passages
Analogs of Phencyclidine (PCP) (Hallucinogens)	PCP PCE TCP	White powder	Taken orally Injected Smoked

The preceding material was reprinted from *What Works: Schools Without Drugs*, a publication of the U.S. Department of Education.

designer drugs. These drugs can be several hundred times stronger than the drugs they are designed to imitate.

The narcotic analogs can cause symptoms such as those seen in Parkinson's disease: uncontrollable tremors, drooling, impaired speech, paralysis, and irreversible brain damage. Analogs of amphetamines and methamphetamines cause nausea, blurred vision, chills or sweating, and faintness. Psychological effects include anxiety, depression, and paranoia. As little as one dose can cause brain damage. The analogs of phencyclidine cause illusions, hallucinations, and impaired perception.

RESOURCES AND ORGANIZATIONS

TOLL-FREE INFORMATION

Al-Anon Family Groups (1-800-356-9996). Provides information on local support groups for adult children of alcoholics (Al-Anon), and teenage children of alcoholics (Alateen). New York and Canada call 212-245-3151.

Cocaine Helpline (1-800-COCAINE). A round-the-clock information and referral service. Reformed cocaine addict counselors answer the phones, offer guidance, and refer drug users and parents to local public and private treatment centers and family learning centers.

The National Federation of Parents for Drug Free Youth (NFP) (1-800-554-KIDS). A national information and referral service that focuses primarily on preventing drug addiction in children and adolescents. NFP refers the caller to a "state networker" or a member group in the caller's community, to help provide assistance to anyone concerned about someone using alcohol or drugs. Call between 9:00 A.M. and 5:00 P.M. (Eastern time).

National Institute on Drug Abuse (NIDA)/U.S. Department of Health and Human Services (1-800-638-2045). A national information service that provides technical assistance to individuals and groups wishing to start drug prevention programs. Currently, the program focuses on the establishing of "Just Say No to Drugs" clubs.

National Institute on Drug Abuse (NIDA) hot line (1-800-662-HELP). A confidential information and referral line that directs callers to cocaine abuse treatment centers in the local community. Free materials on drug abuse are also distributed in response to inquires.

Parents' Resource Institute for Drug Education (PRIDE) Drug Information Line (1-800-241-9746). A national resource and information center, PRIDE refers concerned parents to parent groups in their state or local area, gives information on how parents can form a group in their community, provides telephone consulting and referrals to emergency health centers, and maintains a series of drug information tapes that callers can listen to, free of charge, by calling after 5:00 P.M.

FREE CATALOGS OF DRUG ABUSE PUBLICATIONS
Comp Care Publications (1-800-328-3330). A source for pamphlets, books, and charts on drug and alcohol abuse, chemical awareness, and self-help.

Hazelden Educational Materials (1-800-328-9000). A source for pamphlets and books on drug abuse and alcoholism and curriculum materials for drug prevention.

SCHOOL AND COMMUNITY RESOURCES
Alcohol and Drug Abuse Education Program/U.S. Department of Education. The "School Team" approach offered in this program is designed to enable local schools to prevent and reduce drug and alcohol abuse and associated disruptive behaviors. Five regional centers now provide training and technical assistance to local school districts. For information, write to the U.S. Department of Education, Alcohol and Drug Abuse Education Program, 400 Maryland Avenue SW, Washington, DC 20202-4101.

American Council on Drug Education (ACDE) (301-984-5700). ACDE organizes conferences; develops media campaigns; reviews scientific findings; publishes books, a quarterly newsletter, and education kits for physicians, schools, and libraries; and produces films. For information write to ACDE, 5820 Hubbard Drive, Rockville, MD 20852.

Committees of Correspondence, Inc. (617-774-2641). This organization provides a newsletter and emergency news flashes that give extensive information on issues, ideas, and contacts. Provides a resource list and sells many pamphlets. Membership is $15. For information write to Committees of Correspondence, Inc., 57 Conant Street, Room 113, Danvers, MA 09123.

Families in Action (404-325-5799). This organization maintains a drug information center with more than 100,000 documents. Publishes *Drug Abuse Update,* a sixteen-page newsletter containing abstracts of articles published in medical and academic journals and newspapers throughout the nation. Cost is $10 for four issues. For information write to Families in Action, 3845 North Druid Hills Road, Suite 300, Decatur, GA 30033.

Narcotics Education, Inc. (617-774-2641). This organization publishes pamphlets, books, teaching aids, posters, audiovisual aids, and prevention magazines. Also publishes useful classroom magazines: *Winner* for preteens and *Listen* for teens. For information write to Narcotics Education, Inc., 57 Conant Street, Room 113, Danvers, MA 09123.

National Federation of Parents for Drug Free Youth (NFP) (Washington, D.C., 202-585-KIDS or toll free hot line 1-800-554-KIDS). This national umbrella organization helps parent groups get started and stay in contact. Publishes a newsletter, legislative updates, resource lists for individuals and libraries, brochures, kits, and a *Training Manual for Drug Free Youth Groups.* It sells many books and offers discounts for group purchases. Conducts an annual conference. Membership fees are $15 for an individual; $35 for a group (group membership offers tax-exemption). For information write to NFP, 8730 Georgia Avenue, Suite 200, Silver Spring, MD 20910.

Project 714 (615-622-5714). Offers a plan of action for setting up a student-based, adult-supported program in high schools. Stresses positive peer pressure and prevention, and emphasizes the need to be both drug and alcohol free. Program includes support groups for struggling abusers and for students whose parents or siblings abuse drugs or alcohol. For information write to Project 714, P.O. Box 8936, Chattanooga, TN 37411.

Students Against Driving Drunk (SADD). Stresses that students never drive drunk or drive with someone who has been drinking. Organization has films and videos, copies of the SADD Contract for Life, junior and senior high curriculum, and school starter kits available. For information write to SADD, P.O. Box 800, Marlboro, MA 01752.

Safe Rides. Offers a plan of action for students concerned about fellow classmates who drink and drive. Program involves teenage drivers who, with adult supervision, give weekend rides to students who have been drinking or to students who would otherwise have to ride with someone who has been drinking. For materials on setting up a program send $2 (to cover materials and postage) to Stamford Safe Rides, First United Methodist Church, Cross Road, Stamford, Connecticut 06905.

Target (816-464-5400). Conducted by the National Federation of State High School Associations, Target is an organization of interscholastic activities associations that offers workshops, training seminars, and an information bank on chemical abuse and prevention. A computerized referral service to substance abuse literature and prevention programs began operating in 1987. For information write to National Federation of State High School Associations, 11724 Plaza Circle, P.O. Box 20626, Kansas City, MO 64195.

Toughlove (215-348-7090). This national self-help group for parents, children, and communities emphasizes cooperation, personal initiative, avoidance of blame, and action. It publishes a newsletter and a number of brochures and books, and holds workshops across the country each year. For information write to Toughlove, P.O. Box 1069, Doylestown, PA 18901.

U.S. CLEARINGHOUSES
Publication lists from the following organizations are available on request, along with placement on mailing list for new publications. Single copies are free.

National Institute on Alcoholism and Alcohol Abuse (301-468-2600). Write to NIAAA, P.O. Box 2345, Rockville, MD 20852.

National Institute on Drug Abuse (301-443-6500). Write to NIDA, Room 10-A-43, 5600 Fishers Lane, Rockville, MD 20852.

ADOLESCENT DRUG REHABILITATION PROGRAMS

To find programs for rehabilitating adolescents, call your city or county substance abuse or mental health agency, hospitals, schools, local hot lines listed in the Yellow Pages, and the hot lines listed in this appendix. It is best to visit prospective programs and to talk with people who have completed the program before enrolling.

Listed below are several unique national programs for adolescents, illustrating the wide diversity of long-term intensive treatment available at low cost:

Palmer Drug Abuse Program (PDAP) (915-687-4311). PDAP is a free program supported by private donations and located mainly in southwestern, western, and midwestern States. It accepts out-of-town clients. It is a long-term, out-patient counseling program with day-care capability. It is based on the twelve steps of Alcoholics Anonymous (AA) and uses recuperating substance abusers as peer counselors. The program also maintains parent groups that may be attended by parents who do not have children in the PDAP program. For more information write PDAP National Office, 3300 North A Street, Building 8, Suite 204, Midland, TX 79705.

Straight, Inc. (813-576-8929). Located in selected areas, primarily eastern and midwestern states, the program accepts out-of-town clients. It's a long-term, highly structured outpatient program based on the twelve steps of Alcoholics Anonymous (AA). During the early phase of the program, the new client lives in the home of another teenager who has advanced in the program. This family system provides positive role modeling, close supervision, and a twenty-four hour, drug free environment at low cost. Write Straight, Inc., National Training and Development Center, 3001 Gandy Blvd., P.O. Box 21686, St. Petersburg, FL 33742.

Teen Challenge (717-933-4181). This Christian-oriented residential program has facilities across the country and overseas. It serves young people with a variety of behavior problems besides drug use. Occupational skills are taught. Write Teen Challenge Training Center, Inc., National Office, P.O. Box 198, Rehrersburg, PA 19550.

(Most of these Resources appear in and were reprinted from *What Works: Schools without Drugs,* a U.S. Department of Education booklet.)

APPENDIX THREE

QUESTIONS FOR DISCUSSION

For readers who wish to dig deeper or evaluate their own perspectives in light of what has been said in *What Teenagers Are Saying about Drugs and Alcohol,* here are some questions for discussion:

CHAPTER ONE: TEENAGERS AND DRUGS
1. What are your impressions of drug and alcohol abuse in your own school? In your own community? How do those impressions compare or contrast with the Gallup and *Campus Life* survey statistics presented?
2. Among all the quotes from students, which one quote best reflects how you view the drug and alcohol situation in your school and/or community? Why do you agree with that viewpoint? Which quote do you most disagree with? Why do you disagree?
3. Reread the quotes in "What Do We Discover?" Do you think these students are being honest? Why or why not? Do you agree or disagree with what they say? Why or why not?
4. Did your understanding of why users use change as a result of reading this chapter? Why or why not?
5. If someone uses drugs to escape, what is this individual trying to escape from? What does that tell us about this person?
6. Did you learn anything new about the effects and potential hazards of drug use? If so, what did you discover?

7. Why do you think some people continue to use drugs even when they know the facts?

8. Why do you think some students believe there is such a thing as "responsible drug use"?

9. What happens when we label somebody "druggie" or "stoner"? Why do you think we need to see beyond labels to "the hurting individual within"?

CHAPTER TWO: DRINKS FOR EVERYBODY?

1. Which quote best sums up how you feel about alcohol? Why do you feel this way? Are your feelings about drug use different from your feelings about alcohol use? Why or why not?

2. Which quote do you most disagree with in this chapter? Why do you disagree?

3. Reflect on the "Patterns of Use" chart. Why do students change their minds about alcohol as they get older? What would help people maintain their convictions as they get older?

4. How would you define "peer pressure"? Do you agree or disagree with the author's definition? Why or why not?

5. What do you believe is the main reason teenagers drink? What things should teenagers consider before they go out drinking with their friends?

6. "Don't overdo it" is, for many drinking teenagers, the way to drink responsibly. What does "don't overdo it" mean to you? When thinking through drinking habits and attitudes, why is it important to define what is meant by terms like "don't overdo it"?

7. What is your definition of a casual drinker? Most of the students quoted in this chapter consider themselves casual drinkers. Why are there so many different understandings of what it means to drink casually? Write down the pluses and minuses that you see in being a casual drinker.

8. Did you discover any new ideas about the possible hazards of drinking? What are they?

9. Many students call alcohol a drug. Do you agree or disagree with that definition? How is alcohol like illegal drugs? How is it different from illegal drugs?

10. What part do you think parents and other adults play in a teenager's attitude toward alcohol?

11. Do you think it is inconsistent for adults to be able to drink and for teenagers to be denied that "privilege"? Why or why not?

12. What do you think of the logic that says, "If you are old enough to

get pregnant, fight in a war, and get married, then you are old enough to drink?"

13. Do you think students should be concerned about the drinking habits of other teenagers? Why or why not?

14. Review "Uptight in America?" How are the problems other countries have with alcohol consumption different from our own country's problems? How are those problems like our country's problems?

15. Review "Why Don't We Learn?" Why is it that many students go back to drinking even after they have seen friends or family members hurt or even killed in alcohol-related incidents?

CHAPTER THREE: REASONS NOT TO USE

1. With which arguments against drinking would you agree or disagree? Why?

2. Review the chart, "Comparison of Students from a Religious Background to the General High School Population." How does the information in that chart compare with what you know about students in your school who claim to be Christians? In your church? Why do you think some Christian kids continue to drink regularly—and heavily—when their church standards say no?

3. Review "An Argument against Common Excuses." Do you agree or disagree with the writer of that letter? Why?

4. What types of situations led to the drug and alcohol abuse of each person profiled? What do these reasons for abuse tell us about each of these people?

5. Why do you think it is important to see the person with drug and alcohol problems as an "individual"?

6. Which former abuser did you find most interesting? Why? Do you know anybody like that? What are some ways you could help this person deal with his or her problem?

CHAPTER FOUR: THE ROLES WE PLAY

1. What are the four types of people described? Do you agree with the author's categories? Are there other categories you would add? What are they?

2. Do you believe each one of us should attempt to be a problem solver? Why or why not?

3. Review Adam's story in "Adults: Where Are They?" How did adults hinder Adam's attempt at being a problem solver? Why do you think the

adults acted this way? What would you have done if you had been Adam?

4. How much responsibility should the individual abuser have for his own rehabilitation and change? What should be the problem solver's responsibility to this person?

5. How can a person be a problem solver by just being a friend?

CHAPTER FIVE: HOW DRUGS AND ALCOHOL AFFECT THE INDIVIDUAL

1. How has drug and alcohol abuse affected individuals in your school? Your community?

2. How does addiction happen? Why do addicted people deny they have a problem? Why is it so hard for them to stop using?

3. How is drug addiction like alcohol addiction? How is it different?

4. In this chapter, all of the negatives are discussed. Do you think this analysis is fair? Why or why not?

5. Research and experience tell us that if a teenager comes from a home where there is drug or alcohol abuse, the teenager is quite likely to become an abuser of drugs and/or alcohol. Why do you think this is so? What should a person do if she comes from a home where there is alcohol or drug abuse?

CHAPTER SIX: THE TEENAGE ABUSER AND THE FAMILY

1. What led to Anita's problems?

2. What does the statement "abuse does not occur in a vacuum" mean? If abuse does not occur in a vacuum, what does that say about rehabilitation?

3. What is denial? In what ways is denial a normal part of everyday life? When does denial become unhealthy and destructive? How can we avoid or at least counteract denial when it becomes destructive?

CHAPTER SEVEN: WHAT TO DO?

1. With which quotes in this chapter do you most agree? Why? With which quotes do you most disagree? Why?

2. Many students are in favor of "getting tough" with drug abusers. What can tough legal measures do? What can't tough legal measures do?

3. Why are so many students pessimistic when it comes to changing the drug and alcohol abuse situation?

4. According to what students say in the section "From Pessimism to Healthy Realism," what will help change attitudes toward abuse? Do you agree? How can you work each of these out practically? How can your school? Your community? Your church?

5. What qualities seemed to make Project 714 work?

6. How feasible is a program like Project 714 in your own community? What would you have to do to start one? What obstacles might you face? What kind of commitment would it take on the part of yourself, the entire school, the community, your church?

A STRATEGY FOR HOPE— A PLAN FOR ACTION

While *What Teenagers Are Saying about Drugs and Alcohol* has been an attempt to represent student opinion and offer information, it was also written to motivate individuals to become problem solvers. What follows is a plan for doing that. These ideas will need to be modified to fit specific needs and concerns.

MAKE IT PERSONAL

Review chapter 4. How do you react to the statement that—in one way or another—all people, teenagers and adults, are involved with the issue of drug and alcohol abuse? Evaluate yourself by writing out how you feel about alcohol and drugs, about users of drugs or alcohol, and about what can be done to solve the problem of abuse. Where do you fit in: Active abuser? Struggling Abuser? Bystander? Problem solver?

If you are an active abuser or a struggling abuser it is important to become a problem solver for yourself. See Appendix Two for services that can help you.

If you are bystander, take heart. The fact that you are reading through this strategy says that you want to make positive changes.

If you are a casual drinker, you will probably have to make some serious decisions about your drinking (see "The Casual Drinker" in chapter 2).

If you are a problem solver, you could probably expand your vision. The following points tell you how to do that:

Use your ideas plus this book. Reread chapter 7. What ideas sound good to you? Which ones would work in your school? In your community? In your church? Jot those ideas down, along with any ideas of your own.

Group up. Get together with several of your friends, a concerned group at school, members of your Christian club, or your church youth group. Talk about *What Teenagers Are Saying about Drugs and Alcohol.* Read some quotes that made an impression on you, then talk about the drug and alcohol problem as it relates to your school and community. Next, have each person read chapter 7, then brainstorm ways to become problem solvers in your own school and community. Discuss ways you could work with programs currently in your school (i.e., Students Against Driving Drunk (SADD), Safe Rides, Just Say No club, etc.). Maybe plugging into these groups is the best way for you and your friends to become problem solvers.

Share your ideas with adults. As pointed out in chapter 7, an effective program is one that combines the ideas, talents, and resources (including finances) of both adults and students. Share your ideas with the adults in your life (teachers, youth pastors, youth workers, parents, social workers, etc.).

Refine ideas. There is no way you can do it all at once. Choose two or three goals for the next year. For instance:

- Give two skits on peer pressure to elementary students
- Hold three drug- and alcohol-free parties at the school
- Have a speaker come to talk at an all-school assembly
- Attend a drug and alcohol education conference

Get educated. Appendix Two contains resources for material (a lot of it free) that will help you become better informed about the drug and alcohol abuse problem. Also, study the charts in Appendix One, and the information in chapters 1 and 2.

Get help from those who have been successful. Contact the people at Project 714 for more information to get the people at your school interested and involved. Or ask for information on making Project 714's program work in a church setting. Write to Project 714, P.O. Box 8936,

Chattanooga, TN 37411. Or contact any of the other resources offered in Appendix Two.

Realize the solution will be a long-term venture. Problem solvers and potential problem solvers must realize that attitudes and people change slowly. Don't give up—just take it one step at a time.